Daniel Freeman is Profes[obscured] a National Institute of Healt[obscured] n the Department of Psychia[obscured] is a consultant clinical psychologist in Oxford Health NHS Foundation Trust and a Fellow of University College, Oxford.

Jason Freeman is a writer and editor.

Philippa Garety is Professor of Clinical Psychology at the Institute of Psychiatry, Psychology and Neuroscience, King's College London. She is an honorary consultant clinical psychologist, and Clinical Director and Joint Leader of the Psychosis Clinical Academic Group, in the South London and Maudsley NHS Foundation Trust.

Daniel and Jason have together co-authored several books:

Paranoia: The Twenty-first Century Fear (Oxford, 2008)

Know Your Mind: Everyday Emotional and Psychological Problems and How to Overcome Them (Rodale, 2009)

Use Your Head: The Inside Track on the Way We Think (John Murray, 2010)

Anxiety: A Very Short Introduction (Oxford, 2012)

You Can Be Happy: The Scientifically Proven Way to Change How You Feel (Pearson, 2012)

The Stressed Sex: Uncovering the Truth about Men, Women, and Mental Health (Oxford, 2013)

How to Keep Calm and Carry On: Inspiring Ways to Worry Less and Live a Happier Life (Pearson, 2013)

On Twitter, they are @ProfDFreeman and @JasonFreeman100.

Praise for
Overcoming Paranoid and Suspicious Thoughts,
1st edition

'Everybody is upset from time to time by suspicious thoughts regarding other people's motives. For the first time, the problem of the exaggerated fear of being harmed is laid out in detail. In a clear, engaging style, the authors trace the origins of these fears and tell us what to do about them. This book is essential reading for the large number of people who are plagued by suspicions of other people.'

Aaron T. Beck, University Professor of Psychiatry, University of Pennsylvania and President of the Beck Institute for Cognitive Therapy and Research, USA.

'Although fears and suspicions about others are extremely common and a source of great suffering and social conflict, no book has ever been published to help people deal with such problems. Now finally a group of the world's foremost scientists in the field have come up with a very accessible and readable text providing solutions for those who previously had no source to access.'

Jim van Os, Professor of Psychiatry and Head of University Psychiatric Clinic, Maastricht University Hospital, The Netherlands.

'Until recently the problems caused by suspicious thoughts were greatly underestimated. We had little idea that they were so common, no real sense of what caused them, and no clear strategy for how to tackle them. The authors of this excellent and timely book have played a major role in developing our understanding of how suspicious thoughts arise and, crucially, how we can learn to cope with them. *Overcoming Paranoid and Suspicious Thoughts* is a first-class distillation of their ground-breaking research that will surely establish itself as the best self-help guide on the subject for many years to come.'

Nicholas Tarrier, Professor of Clinical Psychology, Manchester University and Consultant Clinical Psychologist, Manchester Mental Health and Social Care NHS Trust.

'Many of us harbour paranoid and suspicious ideas that have no basis in fact, but it's not something we tend to talk about. This pioneering book shows that, just as many of us can have mild anxiety or depressed feelings without ever requiring specialist help, many of us have minor (but troubling) paranoid thoughts. Most importantly, the book proposes simple and practical ways to understand and overcome these ideas.'

Robin Murray, Professor of Psychiatry, King's College London and Head of the National Psychosis Unit, South London and Maudsley NHS Trust.

'Suspiciousness and irrational fears of being harmed by others are common and distressing experiences, but often go unrecognised. This book is the first to offer practical help to people suffering from this type of difficulty. It is written in a warm and engaging style, aimed at the non-specialist. It will be enormously helpful both to people suffering from suspiciousness and paranoia, and to their friends and relatives.'

Richard Bentall, Professor of Experimental Clinical Psychology and Consultant Clinical Psychologist, Manchester University.

'Feeling depressed, anxious or having an urge to recheck things are universal experiences; in fact they are helpful emotions that motivate us to face up to the day-to-day problems that life throws at us. But they can often escalate and we become aware that they have become our masters and need to be reined in. Suspiciousness is likewise a normal emotion that can serve us well; but overuse it and we can lose the capacity to trust people and soon we are on a slippery slope to isolation and despair. This book is a welcome addition to the self-help literature. It firmly places suspicious thinking in a normal context and offers straightforward, scientifically based guidance to the average man or woman in the street to understand it and to bring it back under control again.'

Max Birchwood, Professor of Mental Health, University of Birmingham and Director of Early Intervention Services, Birmingham and Solihull Mental Health NHS Trust.

The aim of the **Overcoming** series is to enable people with a range of common problems and disorders to take control of their own recovery programme.

Each title, with its specially tailored programme, is devised by a practising clinician using the latest techniques of cognitive behavioural therapy – techniques which have been shown to be highly effective in changing the way patients think about themselves and their problems.

Many books in the Overcoming series are recommended by the UK Department of Health under the Books on Prescription scheme.

Other titles in the series include:

OVERCOMING ANGER AND IRRITABILITY, 2ND EDITION
OVERCOMING ANOREXIA NERVOSA
OVERCOMING ANXIETY, 2ND EDITION
OVERCOMING BODY IMAGE PROBLEMS INCLUDING BODY DYSMORPHIC DISORDER
OVERCOMING BULIMIA NERVOSA AND BINGE-EATING, 2ND EDITION
OVERCOMING CHILDHOOD TRAUMA
OVERCOMING CHRONIC FATIGUE
OVERCOMING CHRONIC PAIN
OVERCOMING COMPULSIVE GAMBLING
OVERCOMING DEPERSONALIZATION AND FEELINGS OF UNREALITY
OVERCOMING DEPRESSION, 3RD EDITION
OVERCOMING DISTRESSING VOICES
OVERCOMING GRIEF
OVERCOMING HEALTH ANXIETY
OVERCOMING HOARDING
OVERCOMING INSOMNIA AND SLEEP PROBLEMS
OVERCOMING LOW SELF-ESTEEM, 2ND EDITION
OVERCOMING MILD TRAUMATIC BRAIN INJURY AND POST-CONCUSSION SYMPTOMS
OVERCOMING MOOD SWINGS
OVERCOMING OBSESSIVE COMPULSIVE DISORDER
OVERCOMING PANIC AND AGORAPHOBIA
OVERCOMING PERFECTIONISM
OVERCOMING PROBLEM DRINKING
OVERCOMING RELATIONSHIP PROBLEMS
OVERCOMING SEXUAL PROBLEMS
OVERCOMING SOCIAL ANXIETY AND SHYNESS, 2ND EDITION
OVERCOMING STRESS
OVERCOMING TRAUMATIC STRESS
OVERCOMING WEIGHT PROBLEMS
OVERCOMING WORRY AND GENERALISED ANXIETY DISORDER, 2ND EDITION
OVERCOMING YOUR CHILD'S FEARS AND WORRIES
OVERCOMING YOUR CHILD'S SHYNESS AND SOCIAL ANXIETY
OVERCOMING YOUR SMOKING HABIT

OVERCOMING PARANOID AND SUSPICIOUS THOUGHTS

2nd Edition

A self-help guide using Cognitive Behavioural Techniques

DANIEL FREEMAN,
JASON FREEMAN &
PHILIPPA GARETY

ROBINSON

First published in Great Britain in 2016 by Robinson

3 5 7 9 10 8 6 4 2

A CIP catalogue record for this book
is available from the British Library.

Important Note
This book is not intended as a substitute for medical advice or treatment. Any person with a condition requiring medical attention should consult a qualified medical practitioner or suitable therapist.

Every effort has been made to trace and contact copyright holders. If there are any inadvertent omissions we apologise to those concerned, and ask that you contact us so that we can correct any oversight as soon as possible.

ISBN: 978-1-47213-594-0

Typeset in Bembo by Initial Typesetting Services, Edinburgh
Printed and bound in Great Britain by Clays Ltd, Elcograf S.p.A.

Papers used by Robinson are from well-managed forests
and other responsible sources

Robinson
An imprint of
Little, Brown Book Group
Carmelite House
50 Victoria Embankment
London EC4Y 0DZ

An Hachette UK Company
www.hachette.co.uk

www.littlebrown.co.uk

Contents

Preface

It has come as something of a shock to this book's authors that it is now ten years since the first edition appeared!

Back in 2006 paranoid and suspicious thoughts were rarely spoken about. When they were discussed it was usually only in connection with mental health problems such as psychosis. But our research had made it clear that paranoia was much more widespread than generally believed: our data suggested that it was probably almost as common as depression or anxiety. Yet we were unable to find a single accessible guide to dealing with suspicious thoughts – which is why we wrote this book!

Today this remains the only self-help book focused on overcoming paranoia. But the prevalence of suspicious thoughts – the fact that they are a normal part of life – is increasingly accepted and understood. And because these thoughts and feelings are talked about more openly, the stigma attached to them has begun to lessen. No one who is troubled by suspicious thoughts need feel ashamed or embarrassed: most of us, at some point in our lives, will experience them.

This new, more open discussion of paranoia has brought a recognition of the role played by social factors. CCTV cameras, to take just one example, send us a not-so-subtle message that the world is a dangerous place. Our media loves to regale us with the details of horrific, bloodthirsty crimes. Public spaces such as train stations and airports remind us to be on our guard for suspicious objects. Small wonder if we're fearful of the people around us!

It has become clearer too that suspicious thoughts aren't just the preserve of adults. As children try to make sense of their often-complicated social world, they too can experience paranoia. Suspicious thoughts (like so many other psychological issues) can begin much earlier in life than was previously understood.

Research over the past decade has shown that genes can play a part in paranoia. Through an accident of birth some of us may be more susceptible to suspicious thoughts than others. But that doesn't mean that people with a genetic vulnerability will inevitably experience problems: far from it. Environmental factors – essentially the things that happen to us in our lives and the way in which we respond to them – are at least as important as genetics.

Then there's the fact that we know much more now about how to treat paranoia, with rigorous clinical trials helping us to pinpoint what works and why. A trial we undertook with 150 patients with severe paranoia, for example, showed that simply limiting the time we spend worrying about suspicious thoughts actually reduces the paranoia. These are insights that can help us all, whether suspicious thoughts are a big problem for us or just an occasional irritant.

This new edition reflects these recent advances in the understanding of paranoia – what it is, why it occurs, and how it can be overcome. We have added new chapters and revised the others, bringing you up to date with the latest scientific developments and presenting even more clinically proven treatment techniques. You'll also find a greater number of personal accounts of paranoia drawn from our website **www.paranoidthoughts.com**.

The structure of the book follows that of the previous edition. In Part One we explain what suspicious thoughts are, how they come about, and what it feels like to experience them. In Part Two we build on this understanding to present ten practical steps to help you cope with your fears. Throughout the book, we use accounts of suspicious thoughts that are based on real-life examples from our clinical practice.

Suspicious thoughts are common, understandable responses to challenging situations. Every day we must decide whether or not to trust other people. In doing so, it's all too easy to misread the intentions of those around us. If paranoia is causing you problems, we want you to take heart from the knowledge that it can be conquered. You *can* get the better of your fears.

Work through the chapters in this book one by one. Follow the programme of techniques that have helped so many people. You'll learn to understand your suspicious thoughts – and to overcome them.

PART ONE

UNDERSTANDING SUSPICIOUS THOUGHTS

1

What do we mean by 'suspicious thoughts about others'?

When I look back on all these worries, I remember the story of the old man who said on his deathbed that he had had a lot of trouble in his life, most of which had never happened.

Winston Churchill

Introduction

It sometimes seems as if the one thing that unites the diverse peoples of the world is our fear of one another. Worries about other people are so common that they seem to be an essential – if unwelcome – part of what it means to be human.

People from a different country; people who do not share our religious or political beliefs or our sexual orientation; even people with an unusual haircut or style of dress – all are frequently the objects of our distrust, anxiety or fear.

And, on a more mundane level, who hasn't worried about walking along a deserted street late at night? Who hasn't fretted, as they approached home after a time away, that they may have been burgled in their absence? Who hasn't found themselves suspecting, perhaps only for a moment, that a friend, colleague or family member hasn't their best interests at heart?

These anxieties may take many different forms, and may vary hugely in degree, but what unites them is the suspicion that *other people intend to do us harm*. There is no doubt that these worries are extremely common among people of all ages, from adolescence to old age. In fact, suspicious and paranoid thoughts may well be as widespread as happy, angry, depressed or anxious thoughts.

We can see evidence of this in the results of the most important survey of mental health in England, the Adult Psychiatric Morbidity Survey (APMS). The survey is carried out every seven years, covers thousands of people, and is designed to be nationally representative – which means it gives us a pretty reliable sense of the mental health of the general population.

The last survey included three questions about paranoid thoughts. Each of these questions focused on the participants' experience over the past year. Asked if they had sometimes felt that people were against them, 19 per cent – or almost one in five – of the participants said that they had. Eight per cent of those questioned reported feeling as though people were deliberately trying to harm them or their interests. And 2 per cent had suspected that a group of people was plotting to cause them serious harm or injury.

It's not only adults who experience paranoid thoughts: children and adolescents are prone too. Indeed, it is when we're young that paranoia (in common with many other psychological problems) often first emerges. In a study of 1,000 UK children aged eight to fourteen, 17.5 per cent said that they felt as though they were a target at school. Almost 12 per cent reported having thought that people had been following or spying on them at school. And 8.4 per cent felt that others at school try to harm them.

There's nothing new about paranoia. Like every other emotion, we can find descriptions dating back many hundreds of years. In 1621, for example, Robert Burton published the best-selling *Anatomy of Melancholy*. Burton wrote the *Anatomy* as part of his efforts to deal with his recurrent and persistent depression (or 'melancholy') – a depression in which paranoid thoughts featured prominently:

> *He [the depressed person] dares not venture alone, for fear he should meet the devil, a thief, be sick; fears all old women as witches, and every black dog or cat he sees he suspecteth to be a devil, every person comes near him is maleficiated [bewitched], every creature, all intend to hurt him.*

Burton continues:

> *Suspicion and jealousy are general symptoms [of depression] . . . If they speak in jest, he takes it in good earnest. If they be not saluted, invited, consulted with . . . they*

think themselves neglected and contemned; for a time that tortures them. If two talk together . . . he thinks presently they mean him . . . Or if they talk with him, he is ready to misconster [misconstrue] every word they speak, and to interpret it to the worst; he cannot endure any man to look steadily at him, speak to him almost . . . He thinks they laugh or point at him . . .

Personal accounts of paranoid thoughts from www.paranoidthoughts.com

Here are just a few of the more than 200 personal accounts of paranoia posted on our website.

I have always been afraid of the dark. As I got older it has progressed. It isn't as much the dark that I'm afraid of now, it's the feeling of what may be in the room that I cannot see. I always feel like someone is there, and is going to either kidnap, rape or kill me. Many times when I am home alone I feel that someone is going to break in and kill me. I always feel that someone is there. I have to look through my entire house in every room and closet to reassure myself that I am truly alone. **Sally**

I am nearly twenty-one and over the last six months I have noticed that I am becoming extremely paranoid of those around me, especially my friends and colleagues at work. All I think about is that they are plotting to screw me over or take advantage of me to better themselves and it's driving me insane! I cannot trust anyone and don't want to talk or interact with anyone. **Nitin**

Whenever I walk down the street I feel like everyone is watching me from inside their houses. When I'm waiting for the bus I think that people are watching me as they drive past in their cars and when I'm on the bus I get the feeling that people are watching me and laughing at me because of my appearance. When I'm waiting for my friends I feel like everyone is walking past and laughing at me because I'm on my own. **Jen**

Last year I thought the FBI was watching me because of a website I visited, even though it was legal. If I saw a helicopter and a police car or a suspicious car near me I would panic, convinced they were coming to get me. That same year I was convinced my new supervisor was plotting to get me fired or demoted. I am chronically suspicious of everyone around me, fearing they're going to attack me or are laughing at me. Living with this black cloud of fear and anger over my head every day really sucks. **Rudy**

I get these strong feelings and thoughts that I am being watched by people at work, all of my family and friends (everyone, basically) and the police including the government! I have grown so used to it now that I don't panic! I hate it so much and it has consumed my whole life. I am not sure why they want to catch me doing something wrong. **Andy**

I always think everyone around me is hostile. Every time I hear people laughing, I always think it's about me and imagine that I've heard them talking and discussing obnoxious things about me. This has led me to isolation and made me painfully shy and afraid of new people. **Paulo**

I thought there was a camera in the lamp-post and a microphone in my button. I thought the cars behind were following me. People at work always seemed to use certain 'phrases' – or I noticed them. Helicopters flew over our house and I was convinced they were spying on us and checking we were at home. I thought the phone was bugged. I really noticed policemen – they seemed to be everywhere and police cars and vans were there because of me. I did not think there was something wrong with my thinking. I thought there was something wrong with society. Why didn't society trust me? I learnt in the end that maybe it was me not trusting myself and maybe I needed to do stuff that I 'approved' of and felt good about. **Tameka**

I feel as if people that are close to me are trying to poison me, and every time I go to dinner there they are giving me more of the poison and soon it will kill me.

I know they wouldn't do it but the feeling is so strong that I feel as if they are. I even feel dizzy whilst eating the food and thinking of the poison. I can't be at home on my own as I feel scared that a ghost, an object or a person is going to kill me. **Katherine**

It's rare to go through life without having a paranoid thought. Like most psychological experiences, there is a spectrum of paranoia within the population: many people have a few, relatively mild paranoid thoughts, while for a few people those thoughts are numerous, persistent and upsetting. How many people get these thoughts frequently? We surveyed over a thousand people to see what proportion regularly experienced suspicious thoughts. Here are a couple of the major discoveries we made:

30–40 per cent of the people we surveyed thought once a week that negative comments about them were being put around.

10–30 per cent thought once a week that they were possibly under threat. That threat tended to be mild (for example, someone's deliberately trying to irritate me) rather than severe (someone has it in for me).

We can see that about a third of the population are regularly bothered by suspicious or paranoid thoughts. (You can find the full details of this survey in the table on page 14.)

These statistics may seem surprising. *I know I've sometimes felt that way*, you may be thinking, *but I had no idea that so many other people have had the same feelings*. One explanation for this surprise may be that most people find it very difficult to talk about these sorts of worries with those closest to them. No one, after all, wants to be seen as anxious or fearful. No one wants to be labelled as 'paranoid'. Even if we do summon the courage to voice our fears, we often dismiss them in the same breath: *I'm probably just being paranoid, but . . .*

In some ways it's hardly surprising that so many of us share these sorts of concerns. More or less every day we must decide whether or not to place our trust in other people. Should we share a confidence? Is it wise to hand over our bank card to the waiter? Are we being reckless when we allow our children to walk home on their own after school?

There's no way around these decisions: they're an inevitable part of life. But they're difficult because it's often so hard to be sure of other people's intentions. Things are made trickier still by the fact that society frequently *encourages* us to be suspicious and fearful. Our newspapers are filled with stories of violent crime. Conspiracy theories abound. Crime has apparently reached such high levels that CCTV cameras are required in every town centre. Governments warn us to be on the lookout for terrorist threats and seek to combat this and other dangers by monitoring our emails and use of the Internet.

We are taught from an early age that the world is a dangerous place. And, of course, in certain contexts it is. Being wary of others is sometimes the most sensible strategy.

However, in this book we don't focus on justified anxieties about others, but rather on *unfounded fears* – fears for which there is no convincing evidence.

Unfounded worries about others don't help us stay safe but instead can bring all manner of distress. Thankfully, these kinds of feelings are not inevitable. In the following pages, you'll learn how to *understand* your unfounded fears. We'll show you how to develop strategies to *cope* with such fears – and, in so doing, how to put an end to any distressing emotions you may be feeling and *move on* with your life.

Throughout the book, we draw on the methods and insights of cognitive behavioural therapy. This approach was first developed as a therapy for depression but has since been used highly successfully to help people deal with a wide range of problems. Cognitive behavioural therapy has been explained by the psychologist Gillian Butler as 'based on the recognition that thoughts and feelings are closely related. If you *think* something is going to go wrong, you will *feel* anxious; if you *think* everything will go fine, you *feel* more confident.' So, if we can understand and change the way we think and the beliefs we hold, we are able to change the way we feel and the way we behave. Most importantly, cognitive behavioural therapy is grounded in science. What you're reading in this book is the product of numerous studies carried out specifically to understand suspicious thoughts. Similarly, the techniques we'll show you to overcome your paranoia have all been rigorously tested in clinical trials.

In this opening chapter we'll talk in more detail about what suspicious thoughts are – and what they're not. We'll spend a little time distinguishing between helpful and unhelpful suspicions. And we'll help you judge which category your concerns fall into.

Assessing your suspicious thoughts

If you'd like to assess your own suspicious feelings and anxieties, have a look at the questionnaire on page 14. Remember that suspicious thoughts and fears about others are very common. Having them isn't necessarily a sign that you have a 'problem': suspicious thoughts can be a reasonable and sensible response to everyday life. However, if you have any of the thoughts listed below about once a week or more – or if there have been periods in your life when you have had them – then this book is likely to be of particular interest to you.

We gave this questionnaire to 1,200 people as part of the survey we mentioned above. Their responses are summarised in the table on page 16. Using this table you can see the percentage of people who have similar experiences to you. For example, you can see that for the thought 'I need to be on my guard against others', 31 per cent of those surveyed rarely had the thought, 17 per cent had the thought once a month, 21 per cent once a week, 21 per cent several times a week, and 10 per cent once a day.

What are suspicious thoughts?

We could have called this section: 'What are fears about others?' We could also have titled it: 'What are paranoid feelings?' or 'What are persecutory beliefs?'

The feelings we discuss in this book go by a variety of names. As you may already have noticed, we make use of them all in this book. Some of these names may be familiar to you, others less so. You may also feel that some are preferable to others (the term 'paranoia', for example, has negative connotations for many people). If you do find any of the terms we use unhelpful, we apologise and hope that you will understand that we want to reflect all of the many names that people use when they describe these sorts of experience.

So what are suspicious or paranoid thoughts? We use the term to mean:

- The fear of something bad happening.
- The belief that others may intend to cause such an event.

Here are some examples of suspicious thoughts:

> Ian, a twenty-one-year-old engineering student: *Sometimes I may walk down the street and see a group of people standing around talking. If they start laughing as I walk past, I worry that they're actually laughing at me.*

> Keith, a fifty-three-year-old postal worker: *I feel that people – particularly colleagues at work – hate me and are constantly trying to put me down.*

I get the feeling that . . .	Rarely	Once a month	Once a week	Several times a week	Once a day
I need to be on my guard against others					
Negative comments about me might be being put around					
People deliberately try to irritate me					
I might be being observed or followed					
People are trying to make me upset					
People communicate about me in subtle ways					
Strangers and friends look at me critically					
People might be hostile towards me					
Bad things are being said about me behind my back					

SUSPICIOUS THOUGHTS ABOUT OTHERS

Someone I know has bad intentions towards me					
I suspect that someone has it in for me					
People would harm me if given an opportunity					
Someone I don't know has bad intentions towards me					
There is a possibility of a conspiracy against me					
People are laughing at me					
I am under threat from others					
I can detect coded messages about me in the press/TV/radio					
My actions and thoughts might be controlled by others					

I get the feeling that . . .	Rarely	Once a month	Once a week	Several times a week	Once a day
I need to be on my guard against others	31%	17%	21%	21%	10%
Negative comments about me might be being put around	35%	24%	21%	14%	7%
People deliberately try to irritate me	57%	17%	15%	8%	4%
I might be being observed or followed	67%	14%	8%	7%	4%
People are trying to make me upset	72%	16%	7%	4%	1%
People communicate about me in subtle ways	52%	22%	14%	9%	3%
Strangers and friends look at me critically	29%	23%	21%	18%	9%
People might be hostile towards me	45%	27%	16%	9%	4%
Bad things are being said about me behind my back	45%	25%	15%	11%	4%

Someone I know has bad intentions towards me	71%	16%	6%	4%	2%
I suspect that someone has it in for me	83%	9%	4%	2%	2%
People would harm me if given an opportunity	83%	9%	4%	2%	2%
Someone I don't know has bad intentions towards me	82%	10%	3%	3%	2%
There is a possibility of a conspiracy against me	90%	5%	2%	1%	2%
People are laughing at me	41%	26%	19%	9%	6%
I am under threat from others	76%	13%	5%	3%	2%
I can detect coded messages about me in the press/TV/radio	96%	2%	1%	1%	1%
My actions and thoughts might be controlled by others	81%	10%	3%	3%	2%

Emily, a thirty-four-year-old solicitor: *I was at a party recently and the thought crossed my mind that some people there were saying negative things about me behind my back.*

Cameron, a twenty-six-year-old photographer: *My ex-girlfriend's family are persecuting me; they make me hear voices and they want me to disappear.*

These four experiences are very different from each other in several ways: for instance the people suspected of harmful intentions; the nature of that harm; and the frequency of the suspicious thoughts.

The experience of persecutory beliefs also varies hugely in severity. Ian's experience is probably something all of us have been through at one time or another; Cameron's feelings are characteristic of someone whose difficulties with these sorts of worries have led him to seek clinical assistance and are less common. (As in Cameron's case, the most severe experiences of persecutory beliefs may be accompanied by what we call **auditory hallucinations** – the experience of 'hearing voices' – that we'll discuss in more detail in Chapter 2.)

Though most of us will have these worries at some point in our lives, they affect us in different ways. The level of distress will vary, as will the certainty with which we hold the belief and the extent to which it preoccupies us. Such worries also vary in plausibility: for example, the worry that people are talking behind your back is, in most cases, probably more plausible (though not necessarily more justified) than the worry that Mossad are planning to kidnap us.

Generally our fears increase in severity the greater our belief in them; our preoccupation; our distress; their implausibility to others. For the great majority of us, our worries about others will be relatively non-severe.

As you can see from the examples above, our worries about others take all sorts of forms, arise in all sorts of situations, and cause varying degrees of distress. But research by psychologists has shown that our fears can be analysed in terms of four **elements of harm**. These four elements are:

- **The perpetrators;**
- **The type;**
- **The timing;**
- **The motivation.**

The following sections use examples to provide a little more detail about each of the elements. As you read the sections, you may find it helpful to consider your own anxieties in these terms.

> Doreen is a fifty-eight-year-old shop worker from London: *At work, if I am restocking the shelves and other staff members are nearby, I sometimes think they are joking and talking about me, but I know they aren't really.*
>
> Chris, a twenty-six-year-old teacher: *Standing at a bus stop at night when I was back in Liverpool, a group*

of drunken youths were walking towards me, and I was worried they may be intent on causing trouble, or they may try to hurt me.

Serena, a twenty-four-year-old musician from Bristol: *I once thought a housemate was trying to steal my possessions as I often caught her standing in the corridor near my room and nowhere near her own room. I got really wound up about this and ended up locking some of my valuables in the garden shed. After this, I began to have other thoughts – like she was trying to poison me because she was always asking me to eat food that she had made and giving me new foreign alcohol to try.*

Eddie, a forty-two-year-old lorry driver and former soldier from Scotland: *For a while I used to believe that MI5, Mossad and the police were trying to kidnap and torture me.*

Kelly, a thirty-nine-year-old mother of three: *I feel that a neighbour is intent upon entering my house and stealing my property.*

Jay, a nineteen-year-old student: *If I'm with a friend and someone rings them on their mobile and they tell the caller they're with me, well if the caller then says something I can't hear and the friend I'm with laughs, I always think that the person on the other end of the phone said something horrible about me.*

Solomon, a thirty-four-year-old journalist: *I am fearful that my family is trying to physically harm me.*

The perpetrators

As the examples above demonstrate, we can suspect absolutely anyone of wanting to do us harm. For Doreen, the perpetrators were her colleagues at work. Serena suspected her housemate. Solomon worried about the intentions of his family, while for Eddie the perpetrators were members of the police force and other governmental organisations. Sometimes we don't know the identity of the people we fear: all we have is a sense of threat. But even if we don't know who it may be, all persecutory beliefs have as a central element the notion of a *perpetrator.*

The type of threat or harm

By harm we don't simply mean physical injury. The exact type of the harm we fear varies enormously. Here are some common types:

- The feeling that we are being *watched* or being *talked about* (Doreen's and Jay's anxieties are of this type).
- The worry that people are using *hints and double meanings* to threaten you without anyone else noticing. For example Sarah, a thirty-one-year-old marketing executive, described how, at a reunion of old friends, someone had made repeated references to a trip to France they'd

all been on as teenagers. She worried that this was actually a coded reference to an embarrassing event that had occurred to her on the trip, and about which she had told no one. She saw the comments as an implicit threat to reveal her secret.

- The fear of being *physically harmed* – for example, attacked, poisoned, even killed. Chris worried about being attacked by youths while out at night; Solomon, whose fears were expressed during clinical treatment, feared that his family wanted to physically harm him.
- *Social harm* – we may, for example, worry about looking bad in the eyes of others; we may suspect that rumours are being spread about us; or we may feel that we are being excluded or ridiculed (Jay's experience is a good example of this).
- We may feel that others are trying to annoy or upset us. Sanjay, a forty-year-old salesman who came to us for treatment, complained that other people were constantly trying to irritate him by such small means as coughing or dragging their feet when they walked. We call this *psychological harm*.
- The fear of being *financially harmed*, or of *damage to our possessions* (Serena, for example, believed that her housemate was trying to steal her property).

- We worry that people want to *get rid of us* – for example, by trying to get us dismissed from our job. Alice, a thirty-eight-year-old college lecturer, told us that she believed colleagues were trying to undermine her by spreading malicious rumours in order to have her removed from her post.
- People with severe persecutory thoughts may feel that their actions or thoughts are being *interfered with* by others. Brian, a fifty-eight-year-old electrician, believed his brain was being tampered with by doctors and ghosts.

The timing of thc threat

When do we believe the harm will happen? By now, you probably won't be surprised to learn that there's no single answer to this question! We may think the harm has already happened or is going on right now: Doreen's anxieties, for instance, arose at the moment when her workmates were gathered nearby. The harm may seem imminent (Chris worried that he was about to be attacked), or likely to occur in the near future (remember Kelly's anxieties about her neighbour). On the other hand, the timescales may be much greater, with the harm seemingly months or even years away. And it's not uncommon for a combination of timings to be involved: we may believe that harm has occurred, is continuing to occur, and will occur again in the future.

The motivation for the harm

Why do we think we are a target for harm? What do we feel we've done to deserve this ill will on the part of others?

Sometimes there's a feeling that we're simply *victims* – that we've done nothing to deserve the threat or persecution we perceive. Take, for example, the case of Hugh, a sixty-one-year-old retired civil servant. He commented:

> *Seeing a group of youths makes me feel awkward – especially because you know they are more than likely to try to impress their peers. As a result, you realise you may be a victim of their youth and peer pressure.*

In other cases we may suspect that we're at risk because of *who we are*. If we think of ourselves as popular and successful, we may feel that we're being threatened because others are jealous of our achievements. If we have a negative view of ourselves – for instance, if we feel uncomfortable in social situations – we may feel that others notice this and pick on us.

Lastly, we may believe that the threat is provoked by *something we've done*. We may feel that we're being rightly punished for a serious mistake or misdemeanour, or our actions may be relatively minor: Majid, a twenty-one-year-old student from Bristol, explained his worries in these terms:

Because I won't take part in some activities that everyone is doing and I decide to stand out and not give in to peer pressure, I think that they talk behind my back

In the last few pages we've seen just how varied our fears about others are. And yet they share four common elements – what we might describe as four structuring principles. No matter how diverse the content of our fears may be, the elements or principles remain remarkably constant.

We're almost there in our attempt to pin down what we mean by suspicious thoughts. But we need to take one last step. Before we can be absolutely clear about what suspicious thoughts are, we need to examine *what they're not*.

What suspicious thoughts are not

Suspicious thoughts can resemble two other types of psychological experience: *social anxiety and shyness* and *post-traumatic stress disorder.*

Social anxiety and shyness involve a fear of social situations and there can be hardly anyone who hasn't experienced this at some point in their life. We worry that the people around us will think negatively of us – that they'll think we're boring, or stupid, or out of place. And if they feel this way about us, we reason, they'll naturally dislike and avoid us.

You may have noticed that social anxiety and shyness resemble persecutory anxiety, particularly if that persecutory anxiety focuses on fears of *social harm*. Persecutory thoughts often revolve around the anxiety caused by social situations – as we've seen, social situations are perhaps the most common context for such worries. With persecutory thoughts, just as with social anxiety and shyness, we worry about being embarrassed, humiliated or rejected by others.

But there's one very important difference between them; social anxiety and shyness don't involve us feeling that others *deliberately intend* to make us feel foolish or rejected. Central to the experience of persecutory ideas, on the other hand, is the belief that other people *want to harm us*.

Post-traumatic stress disorder (PTSD) is a term used to describe a range of experiences caused by a traumatic event. Any number of events may trigger PTSD – from mugging or rape to a road accident or military battle. We may find ourselves having persistent and intrusive thoughts about the event long after it's occurred. We may undergo flashbacks, when it seems as if the event is happening again.

Such experiences tend to be highly distressing, so much so that we avoid any situation associated with the traumatic event. Christopher is a barrister. He was the victim of a violent mugging one evening on a street near his London home. Over time, his fears about being attacked again led him to avoid leaving the house, especially after dark.

As with social anxiety and shyness, PTSD seems to overlap with persecutory thoughts. With both, we may fear other people and believe that they are going to hurt us. PTSD, however, is characterised by the strong *link to a traumatic event*.

Like persecutory thoughts, social anxiety and PTSD can be helped by cognitive behavioural therapy. Our list of recommended reading in Appendix 2 includes some excellent titles on the subject and, if you or people you care about are affected by these experiences, we urge you to consult them.

Suspicious thoughts can be good for you!

But aren't we *right* to be suspicious of others?

The world is, after all, sometimes a dangerous and hostile place. From an early age we are taught to be vigilant. As we grow older this teaching is reinforced by, for example, the media, or politicians, or – as often as not – simply by those around us. The list of those who want to harm us in some way seems to increase by the day: pickpockets, muggers, burglars, child abductors, drug dealers, terrorists. We learn at an early age not to accept lifts from strangers. As we get older, we understand that we should keep hold of our belongings when in a public place. We choose our route carefully when walking home at night. At ATM machines we develop a clever routine of entering our PIN codes and withdrawing our money as quickly and as surreptitiously as possible. Such behaviour is utterly sensible.

Is it really so odd to worry about being secretly monitored by others? Aren't our town centres full of CCTV cameras? Don't many of the world's governments have powers to intercept our phone calls, letters and email? And we have to be realistic: not everyone can be trusted – sometimes not even our family and friends.

Given all this, being wary about the intentions of others seems highly prudent. And it often is. On the other hand, suspicious thoughts can also be a negative influence in our lives, as we'll consider in the following section.

When suspicious thoughts are unhelpful

Think back to the comments made earlier by Keith and Emily. Keith felt that he was hated by the people around him, and particularly by his colleagues at work. He thought they were constantly trying to put him down. Emily told of how she'd felt that the other people at the party she was attending were saying negative things about her behind her back.

Both Keith and Emily may have been absolutely right. But there are other possibilities. Their fears may have been exaggerated: for instance, Keith may not have been the most popular person in his office, but no one hated him and no one was trying to harm him in any way. Or their anxieties may have been unjustified: Emily saw people talking to one another, as they always do at parties, but there was no evidence to suggest they were talking about her. And this is when suspicious thoughts become unhelpful: when they are *exaggerated or unrealistic*.

When suspicious thoughts are unfounded they no longer help us protect ourselves. Instead, we tend to spend a lot of time worrying about our particular fears and anxieties, at the expense of other more positive elements in our life. And this preoccupation is often accompanied by distress. For example, Emily's experience at the party caused her to think twice about attending such social gatherings in the future. But avoiding these situations didn't help: instead, the lack of social contact made her feel lonely and unhappy.

Keith began to hate going to work and felt anger toward the colleagues he thought were out to get him. Indeed, he began to withdraw from social situations as a whole. But staying at home didn't make his anger disappear. It also brought about a sense of isolation and depression.

Keith's is a relatively severe experience. For many of us, the distress caused by our unfounded worries about others isn't as pronounced. But it is real and it is damaging. The good news, however, is that it is not inevitable. As the following chapters will demonstrate, we can do something about it.

How can we tell whether our suspicious thoughts are justified?

We've seen that worries about others are very common and are often sensible. We've also learned that unjustified worries can have a negative impact on our life and emotions. So how can we tell whether our worries are justified or not?

Well, it's not always easy, as you may have discovered. Emily may have suspected others at the party of talking about her behind her back, but how could she prove or disprove this? Keith may have found himself assigned to what he considered to be less interesting work at the post office. But how would he ever know for sure whether this happened because he was disliked by his colleagues, or whether it was simply because the department needed to reorganise?

The obvious answer in both Keith and Emily's cases may seem to be to *talk to the people concerned*. But this is often really difficult. Even raising our worries with friends and family can be a big challenge. It can feel like a confession of weakness – an embarrassing sign that we can't cope. Sometimes, though, that embarrassment is itself a sign that we suspect our fears might be exaggerated. Opening up to others is hard, but if we don't do it we never get another perspective on our worries; we never get the chance to discuss our fears with another person.

If you're struggling to decide whether your suspicious thoughts are justified, ask yourself the following questions:

Eleven key questions

1. Would other people think my suspicions are realistic?
2. What would my best friend say?
3. Have I talked to others about my worries?
4. Is it possible that I have exaggerated the threat?
5. Is there any indisputable evidence for my suspicions?
6. Are my worries based on ambiguous events?
7. Are my worries based on my feelings rather than indisputable evidence?
8. Is it very likely that I would be singled out above anyone else?
9. Is there any evidence that runs contrary to my suspicions?
10. Is it possible that I'm being at all over-sensitive?

11. Do my suspicions persist despite reassurance from others that they are unfounded?

There are no hard and fast rules for deciding for certain whether a worry is realistic. But by asking yourself these questions you can determine the *probability* of the suspicion being justified.

The probability that your fears are *unrealistic* increases the more you feel that:

> No one else fully shares your suspicions;
>
> There is no indisputable evidence to support your worries;
>
> There is evidence against your suspicions;
>
> It is unlikely that you would be singled out;
>
> Your fears persist despite reassurance from others;
>
> Your fears are based on feelings and ambiguous events.

Assessing whether or not your fears are realistic is the first step towards achieving the balance we're all aiming for: *being suspicious only when appropriate.*

Chapter summary

- By **suspicious thoughts** we mean the worry that other people intend to cause us harm.
- Such thoughts are extremely common, though they're rarely talked about.
- Suspicious thoughts vary enormously in severity and in content, but it can be helpful to analyse them in terms of their common elements: the perpetrator of the harm; the nature of the harm; the timing of the harm; and the motivation for the harm.
- Suspicious thoughts can resemble social anxiety and post-traumatic stress disorder, though in fact they are different in certain key aspects.
- In certain circumstances suspicious thoughts can be helpful.
- Unhelpful suspicious thoughts are those that are exaggerated or unrealistic.
- It is often hard to decide whether your suspicions are justified but asking yourself certain key questions can help.

2

When do we experience paranoid and suspicious thoughts?

'I am not so unreasonable, sir, as to think you at all responsible for my mistakes and wrong conclusions; but I always supposed it was Miss Havisham.'

'As you say, Pip,' returned Mr Jaggers, turning his eyes upon me coolly, and taking a bite at his forefinger, 'I am not at all responsible for that.'

'And yet it looked so like it, sir,' I pleaded with a downcast heart.

'Not a particle of evidence, Pip,' said Mr Jaggers, shaking his head and gathering up his skirts. 'Take nothing on its looks; take everything on evidence. There's no better rule.'

Charles Dickens *Great Expectations*

Introduction

One of English literature's best-loved novels is Charles Dickens's *Great Expectations*. It follows the fortunes from childhood to young adulthood of Philip Pirrip (known to all as 'Pip'), a village boy brought up by his bad-tempered sister and her much more likeable blacksmith husband. As the novel reaches its conclusion, we come to see – just as Pip eventually sees for himself – that Pip has misunderstood almost all of the major events and people of his life.

For example, when an unknown person makes Pip suddenly rich he assumes that his benefactor is the deranged but apparently wealthy Miss Havisham. He's wrong. Miss Havisham is no one's benefactor; she lives in a mansion, certainly, but she has no money. When Miss Havisham brings together Pip and her beautiful protégée Estella, Pip falls deeply in love. He does not see that Estella has been so corrupted by Miss Havisham that she can bring him (and herself) only misery.

The list of misunderstandings is a long one! Pip believes not only that the middle-class world he's moving into is superior to the modest village life he's leaving behind, but also that the people in that middle-class world are superior too. He is mistaken on both counts, an error which leads him to abandon the one person in the world who truly loves him: his blacksmith stepfather Joe Gargery. And when Pip encounters the escaped convict Magwitch he feels fear, repulsion and shame. He has no idea that Magwitch is in fact his mysterious benefactor.

Pip is a master of misinterpretation. Again and again he makes the wrong judgement, draws the wrong conclusion. But we shouldn't be too hard on him. For us all, understanding the true meaning of the events and emotions we experience can sometimes be bewilderingly difficult. As *Great Expectations* demonstrates, life can be extraordinarily ambiguous. It's not surprising that we occasionally misinterpret things. And our preconceptions, preferences and – let's be honest! – our prejudices don't always help us deal with that ambiguity.

You may be wondering what all this has to do with the subject of this chapter: when do we experience suspicious thoughts? In the next few pages we'll look at the typical situations in which suspicious thoughts commonly occur. We'll see that they are often sparked into life by things around us. We'll see too that suspicious thoughts are also frequently related to the way we are feeling inside. But whether the trigger for our fears seems to come from outside (what we might call the external world) or inside (our internal state), those fears reflect our interpretation of what's happening. In trying to make sense of our experiences, we make judgements and develop explanations – just like Pip.

We think – and you may well do so too – that persecutory thoughts don't just occur out of the blue. *They are our attempts to make sense of our experiences.* They are our explanations of the world around us or the way we feel inside. As you read this chapter think about the situations in which you experience suspicious thoughts. Often there are one or two specific details that trigger our suspicions. As preparation for the suggestions we make later in the book for dealing with your fears, try to identify exactly what it is in these situations that you find troubling. Ask yourself these questions: *What sorts of situations trigger my fears? What is it about these situations that seems threatening?*

When do we experience suspicious thoughts?

There are two main types of trigger for suspicious thoughts:

- The situations, events and experiences we encounter in the world;
- The way we feel inside.

We call these **external** and **internal** triggers. Some people's fears are triggered by just one specific experience; for other people their fears may be provoked by a range of situations. We'll start by looking at some common external triggers.

External triggers

Suspicious thoughts often arise when:

- We're in social situations;
- We're in situations from which it is difficult to escape;
- We feel exposed;
- We think we might be blamed, accused, mocked or criticised;
- Unusual events occur;
- We're alone.

Let's explore each of these in more detail.

Social situations

I was at a party recently and the thought crossed my mind that some people there were saying negative things about me behind my back . . . I could see a group of people I knew from work chatting together on the other side of the room. I saw them look in my direction a couple of times and then immediately look away. I thought they were maybe feeling guilty or embarrassed about discussing me and that's why they looked away. Later I heard them laughing and wondered whether they were laughing at me.

These comments from Emily, the solicitor we met in Chapter 1, are a good illustration of the ways in which social situations (such as parties or meetings) can trigger suspicions about others. For many of us, social situations can be stressful events. We may feel a pressure to fit in with the other people there. It can seem as though we're forced to perform. We have to try to be entertaining, amusing, articulate – even just plain polite – when really we'd prefer to be almost anywhere else in the world doing just about anything else!

In situations that provoke these kinds of anxieties, it's not surprising that we may interpret what's going on around us negatively. Like Emily, we worry that the laughter we hear is at our expense. If we spot people looking at us while chatting to someone else we wonder – just like Emily – whether they're talking about us. We overhear snatches of conversation and can't help feeling that they might relate to us, that rumours are being spread about us. If people don't come up to talk to us, we may assume it's because no one likes us. Even if we are part of a group chatting, other worries can arise. Emily told us:

> *Sometimes at parties I'd find myself feeling very distant from the group of people I was talking to. It seemed like I had nothing to contribute to the conversation. Even when I did have something I wanted to say, the people I was with didn't seem to want to hear it. Then I'd worry that, because I couldn't join in with the conversation, the others would think I was stupid. I'd think: I don't belong here.*

I don't fit in. Sometimes (and this seems very odd!), I'd almost feel as if I weren't there at all – like I'd somehow vanished.

These kinds of anxieties naturally make it very difficult for us to enjoy the occasion. And amidst all the stress, amidst all the troubling little details of the evening – the comment overheard, the glance from a colleague – is the sense that it's so hard to be sure whether what we've noticed is really going on or not. This feeling of uncertainty is common to all the situations we're going to look at in this chapter. We rarely know for sure whether someone means us harm. It's worth keeping this crucial point in mind as you read the following sections – and it's worth thinking too about its relevance to your own experiences.

Situations from which it's difficult to escape

I sometimes find journeys on public transport difficult. If someone looks at me, it can feel like they're weighing me up. I don't know why. And when they look away – back down to their book or tablet or whatever – it's as though they can't bear to look at me any more. If the seat next to me is free, and someone gets on, if they don't take the seat it makes me feel as though there's something wrong with me. I look at the person they're sitting next to and wonder why they chose that person and not me. Other times someone might be sitting next to me and it feels like they've done it deliberately to crowd my space – they're

> *leaning into me or rustling their paper really loudly or something. Once I was on the train and the guy next to me was coughing every five seconds. It felt like he was doing it on purpose to annoy me, even though I knew he wasn't.*

These comments from Melissa, a twenty-three-year-old student from London, capture perfectly the sort of persecutory thoughts that can be triggered when we're stuck somewhere for a while. Bus and train journeys are typical examples of this, and you might have had similar experiences in lifts or on car journeys with friends or family.

For Samuel, a thirty-year-old journalist, crowded cinemas could provoke these kinds of worries:

> *I'd feel trapped. I hated the embarrassment of having to ask so many people to move in order to escape. I could feel myself becoming more and more uptight. Sometimes I got really panicky. The sound of the film suddenly seemed deafening. I couldn't bear to look at the screen because the colours were so intense. I felt like speaking to the manager – they were screening the film in some weird way for some weird reason. What were they trying to do to us? If someone opened a bag of sweets three rows away it sounded like an explosion! If someone whispered to their companion, I'd hear it as loud as if they were yelling through a megaphone! And I'd think they were maybe doing it deliberately to annoy me.*

Situations in which we feel exposed

Being out and about can sometimes make us feel very vulnerable. Alone, and out of reach of the safety of home, our perception of the world and the people around us changes. Suddenly, it can seem as if we are surrounded by potential danger. In Chapter 1 we heard from Ian, a twenty-one-year-old engineering student. He told us:

> *Sometimes I may walk down the street and see a group of people standing around talking. If they start laughing as I walk past, I worry that they're actually laughing at me. I tend to deal with this by trying to hurry past them. I make sure I don't look at them in case I draw more attention to myself. If someone bumps into me, I wonder whether they did it deliberately.*

It's a fair bet that we've all felt like this from time to time, particularly when walking home alone at night. Sharon is a forty-one-year-old mother of three. Her comments provide another insight into the worries that feeling exposed can provoke:

> *If I'm in town – in a shop or something – and someone looks at me, I might wonder what they're up to. There are times when – for some reason – I find all sorts of things suspicious: someone sitting on a bench, someone talking on a mobile phone, even someone wearing sunglasses when it isn't very sunny. If they look in my direction, I think there must be a reason and that it*

> *may involve me – maybe they're planning something. In the park the other day some kids were messing around and yelling really loudly. I thought, they're doing it on purpose to annoy me. Actually, I don't think they'd even noticed I was there!*

Just like our other examples of situations in which we can feel suspicious, when we feel exposed relatively insignificant details in the world around us – for example, the fact that someone is sitting on a bench – can suddenly seem important signs that someone means us harm.

Situations in which we might be blamed, accused, mocked or criticised

In Chapter 1 we mentioned Sarah, a thirty-one-year-old marketing executive. Sarah was worried that, at a reunion of old friends, people were dropping unkind hints about an embarrassing event that had happened to her on a school trip to France:

> *I'd gone into a supermarket to buy some chocolate as a present for my grandmother. I ended up with a trolley full of stuff! But while I was shopping, I decided – why, I've no idea – to see if I could sneak something past the cashier. I'd never stolen anything before that and I've never stolen anything since. Anyway, I put my bag in the trolley and hid a packet of sweets underneath it. I thought I'd be able to push the trolley past the cashier*

> *without her noticing the sweets. But I was just about to pay when the woman behind me noticed the sweets. I don't know whether she or the cashier knew what I was up to. They were very pleasant and acted as if I must have just forgotten the sweets. But I felt awful – I still feel awful about it – and I couldn't wait to get out of there. I never told anyone about what had happened.*

Doing something wrong – or just feeling as though we have – is frequently a trigger for persecutory thoughts. The actual deed may well be a very minor one – a malicious thought, a mistake at work, or (as in Sarah's case) a youthful indiscretion. But we worry that other people know about it and dislike and even punish us for it. We may feel that, though we've told no one about our mistake, the sense of guilt and shame is plain to see on our face. It can seem, as it did to Sarah, that the consequences of our actions will last for years.

But sometimes it's not the fact that we've done something wrong that provokes persecutory thoughts – it's simply the feeling that we're in a situation in which *we might be accused of doing wrong*. This can lead to a powerful sense of vulnerability. And of course it's not just any type of vulnerability: it's specifically vulnerability to accusation, to the mistaken thoughts and actions of others. If something does happen, who will there be to act as a witness to our innocence?

If the mere possibility of accusation can provoke persecutory fears, it's hardly surprising that such fears can also be sparked when *we have actually been criticised or mocked*. In the previous chapter we heard about Alice, a lecturer who believed that there was a plot to remove her from her job. This belief seemed to have its roots in an angry but apparently trivial exchange Alice had had several months before with a colleague in a meeting. The colleague had seemed to criticise the way Alice taught a particular course. This incident left Alice feeling that the colleague was carrying a vendetta against her. Moreover, she worried that others at the meeting who'd witnessed the argument would share the colleague's criticism of her. Every time she saw the colleague – and eventually every time she met someone who'd also been at the meeting – her anxiety seemed to grow.

When unusual events occur

Earlier in this chapter Sharon told us:

> *There are times when – for some reason – I find all sorts of things suspicious: someone sitting on a bench, someone talking on a mobile phone, even someone wearing sunglasses when it isn't very sunny.*

Wearing sunglasses on a cloudy day might seem to many of us an odd thing to do, but for Sharon it's more than odd: it's a sign of possible threat. Like Sharon, many people who experience suspicious thoughts find them triggered by apparently odd or unusual events. Events that are almost certainly coincidental can start to seem connected. We might, for example, worry if we spot the same car behind us at several points in a journey or if we see the same person in the street two or three times. For Serena, the musician we heard from in Chapter 1, finding her flatmate on more than one occasion in the hallway near Serena's bedroom sparked the belief that the flatmate was planning to steal items from her room. She began to feel that things in her room had been disturbed or rearranged, reinforcing her worries about her flatmate. *Unusual events, coincidences and apparent connections* can all make us suspect that there's more going on than meets the eye – and that other people mean us harm.

When we're alone

For many of us it's only when we are alone and reflecting on the day's events that suspicious thoughts occur. Only then do we remember and begin to consider the little details that so often are sufficient to prompt our anxieties. In the previous chapter we heard about the experiences of Keith, who came to feel that his colleagues at the postal sorting office where he worked were hostile to him. Keith told us:

> *It became a habit. I'd get home from work, make myself a cup of tea and try to read the paper or have a nap. But then I'd find myself thinking back through the day. And then all kinds of things that hadn't bothered me at the time – a comment someone had made, a look I thought someone had given me – started to worry me.*

Keith attempted to deal with his anxieties by avoiding work and social situations as much as possible. But isolation can just leave us with more time on our hands to dwell on our worries, while also depriving us of the opportunity to disprove our fears. If we never spend time with the people we think are hostile to us, we never have the chance to find out whether they are or not.

We've spent the preceding few pages outlining the variety of situations that commonly trigger suspicious thoughts. Varied though the situations are, it's often the same types of information that seem to contribute to our anxieties:

- **Non-verbal signs**, such as people's expressions, hand gestures, or the way someone is dressed.
- **Verbal signs**, for example something that is said to us or snatches of conversation we overhear, particularly when we think the comment is unpleasant or when we're not sure who or what it refers to.
- **Coincidences and unusual events**, for example seeing the same car behind us several times throughout a journey or hearing things we've said apparently repeated by someone else.

These kinds of information are almost always ambiguous – they could mean any number of things. And yet we place so much weight on our interpretations. This is natural: like Pip in *Great Expectations* we want to make sense of our experiences. But after a while we may find that our interpretations start to change the way we approach certain situations. If we've felt out of place and awkward at social events, the latest invitation only fills us with dread. If we've come to suspect that a colleague doesn't like us, we're apprehensive every time we have to deal with her. We begin to *expect* to have a negative experience. *We take our explanations of past events and project them on to the future.* The smallest gesture or most offhand comment is enough to confirm our suspicions. Yet the extent to which these events affect us is often highly dependent on *how we feel inside*, and it's these *internal triggers* that we're going to look at now.

Internal triggers

The common internal triggers for suspicious thoughts include:

- Our **emotions** – for example feelings of anxiety, unhappiness, guilt, shame, anger, disgust, and even in some cases elation.
- Feelings of **arousal** – by which we mean a feeling of being especially alert and sensitive.

- Changes in the way we *perceive* the world around us, for example the way things look or sound or smell. We call these sorts of feelings **anomalous experiences**.
- Inebriation through **drugs or alcohol**.

In the following pages we'll look in more detail at each of these.

Our emotions

It probably won't surprise you to learn that we're much less likely to experience suspicious thoughts when we're feeling happy, calm and focused on a task.

In contrast, the most common emotional trigger for feelings of paranoia is **anxiety**. Keith's experiences provide an excellent illustration of this:

> *It got to the stage where I dreaded going to work. I slept badly the night before. I could feel myself tensing up on the journey in. By the time I reached the building I was in a right state: heart pounding, headache, sweating – the lot. I had to really fight the temptation to just turn around and go home. Eventually I gave in to that temptation and stayed away altogether.*

When we're feeling this way, it's much more likely that we'll make negative interpretations of the things that happen to us. After all, it's hard to make cool, calm judgements when we're so tense. Keith's anxiety became the perfect platform for his persecutory fears, making him feel so on edge that any ambiguous behaviour from colleagues was likely to be seen by him as hostile.

The second major emotional trigger is **low mood**. You may remember from Chapter 1 that as far back as the seventeenth century Robert Burton made the link between suspicious thoughts and depression. Low mood is a catch-all term we use for the variety of ways in which we feel down – for instance feeling miserable, sad or depressed; having reduced energy levels or interest in life; or feeling bad about ourselves, maybe because of a sense of shame, or guilt, or the belief that we're alone, or worthless, or unloved, or a failure. As with anxiety, low mood seems to make us susceptible to our fears about others. In some cases, the effect low mood has on our behaviour can prompt the very events that we interpret as suspicious. For example, if we're feeling depressed we may not feel like chatting to friends or colleagues. Other people pick up on this and leave us alone, and we then worry that they are excluding us.

Low mood features in the stories of several of the people we've heard from. In Chapter 1, Jay explained:

If I'm with a friend and someone rings them on their mobile and they tell the caller they're with me, well if the caller then says something I can't hear and the friend I'm with laughs, I always think that the person on the other end of the phone said something horrible about me.

Jay was asked why he thought people were saying horrible things about him:

I don't know . . . I guess I don't have a very high opinion of myself and I expect others to feel the same way about me.

Emily told us about her difficulties in social situations:

I'd worry that, because I couldn't join in with a conversation, the others would think I was stupid. I'd think: I don't belong here. I don't fit in . . . That feeling of not belonging, of being different and isolated, is actually something I've experienced at various times of my life. It comes and goes. I've no idea where it comes from.

The hostility Emily and Jay detect in others reflects the way they feel about themselves. Their persecutory thoughts are able to build on, and take advantage of, their low mood. The way we feel about ourselves appears to have a big influence on how we interpret events – and specifically our sense of how others feel about us. It's as if we're trying to make that leap into the wide world around us – to really understand what's going on – but we keep running into the wall of our emotions.

Two other emotions worth mentioning here are **anger** and **elation**. When we're angry, the little problems and irritations of life seem to have much more of an effect on us. We feel irritated, wound up, on edge. Our fuse is shorter! When we're in a mood like this, suspicious thoughts are more likely to pop into our heads. We may start to feel that the child sitting next to us on the bus is sniffing every thirty seconds just to wind us up even further, or that the man who bumps into us as we get off has done so on purpose.

Elation – a feeling of exceptional happiness – is a less common trigger for persecutory worries, but one that does affect a number of people. With feelings of elation can come a sense that we're different from others, that we're particularly blessed: that we are *special*. We may expect other people to be aware of our specialness and to treat us accordingly. When we don't receive the recognition we feel we deserve, we may conclude that this is a calculated slight on the part of others – we feel that they're deliberately trying to undermine us.

Feelings of arousal

Let's return to Keith's description of his anxiety at the prospect of going to work:

> *I could feel myself tensing up on the journey in. By the time I reached the building I was in a right state: heart pounding, headache, sweating – the lot. I had to really fight the temptation to just turn around and go home.*

Keith's emotional response to this stressful situation puts him in a state of *arousal.* We use arousal to describe a state of unusual alertness. We might feel our heart beat faster, or have butterflies in our stomach. Our mind is buzzing with thoughts; we feel on edge, perhaps even out of control. Arousal is our body's way of dealing with a potentially dangerous situation. We may not even be conscious of that danger, but our body is gearing up for action.

Arousal is associated with a range of emotions, including those we've just been looking at: anxiety, low mood, anger and elation. But it's not just emotions that can cause arousal: drugs and alcohol can do it, and we'll discuss these later in this chapter. Arousal can be brought about by having to deal with traumatic or highly stressful situations (for example a bereavement, lack of money, or problems in our relationships). Lack of sleep is another common trigger. Keith's nightmarish journeys to work were frequently preceded by sleepless nights, for instance; and we're all familiar with the very strange feelings that sleeplessness can cause.

All of these experiences can change the way we feel about ourselves and the world, knocking us out of our usual, comfortable stride and *putting us on our guard*. And since arousal is a sign that we sense danger, it's perhaps not surprising that these feelings are often the backdrop to suspicious thoughts in which *other people are the danger.*

Anomalous experiences

Anomalous experiences are closely linked to arousal.

Arousal is our body on edge, sensing danger and preparing to flee or fight. For most of us, arousal is a departure from the norm – we don't usually feel this way. When we're aroused, our bodies, our minds and the world around us can feel very different. Things can appear brighter or more vivid; sounds can seem louder and more intrusive. In fact, any of our senses can be affected. We might become unusually sensitive to smells; objects might seem odd to the touch.

We call these altered perceptions of ourselves and the world *anomalous experiences*. As with arousal, there is a lot of evidence to suggest that we are more prone to the range of anomalous experiences when we've lost someone close, or suffered some other traumatic event, or when we've gone without sleep for an extended period. Anomalous experiences are very common, and are not always unpleasant. Many people are very relaxed about such experiences; indeed, some regard them as life enhancing. But for those who find them stressful, the attempt to make sense of what's going on can trigger suspicious thoughts. Earlier in this chapter, we heard about Samuel's experience in crowded cinemas:

> *I could feel myself becoming more and more uptight. Sometimes I got really panicky. The sound of the film suddenly seemed deafening. I couldn't bear to look at the screen because the colours were so intense. I felt like speaking to the manager – they were screening the film in some weird way for some weird reason. What were they trying to do to us? If someone opened a bag of sweets*

three rows away it sounded like an explosion! If someone whispered to their companion, I'd hear it as loud as if they were yelling through a megaphone! And I'd think they were maybe doing it deliberately to annoy me.

Samuel's claustrophobic anxiety escalates until he's experiencing his surroundings in some very unusual ways. And when he tries to make sense of these experiences, he wonders whether they're caused deliberately by other people.

Other common types of anomalous experience include feeling as though:

- Our thoughts aren't our own.
- Apparently insignificant events are actually highly significant.
- The world isn't real.
- We ourselves don't exist.

Psychologists call this last one depersonalisation, and it's something Emily has sometimes felt at parties:

Sometimes (and this seems very odd!), I'd almost feel as if I weren't there at all – like I'd somehow vanished. I'd feel this especially if I was on my own, or finding it difficult to join in a conversation. I'd be incredibly conscious of all these people laughing and having fun and it seemed like I was just a void in comparison, somehow lightweight and invisible.

Psychologists have identified five types of depersonalisation. Each one is more common in people who are experiencing paranoid thoughts. We also know that depersonalisation (just like paranoia, as we'll see later) can be triggered by worry.

Here are examples of the five types of depersonalisation:

- **Numbing** 'When a part of my body hurts, I feel so detached from the pain that it feels as if it were someone else's pain.'
- **Unreality of self** Feeling as though you're a detached observer of yourself.
- **Perceptual alterations** 'When I touch things with my hands, I can't feel them properly because it seems like it isn't me who is doing the touching.'
- **Unreality of surroundings** 'What I see looks flat and lifeless – as if I were looking at a picture.'
- **Temporal disintegration** 'When I'm in a new situation, it feels as if I have been through it before.'

As you'll have seen from the examples above, anomalous experiences come in a variety of forms. But perhaps the most 'notorious' is *hallucinations* – when we see or hear things that haven't actually occurred. (These sorts of experience are also often referred to as *illusions* or *hearing voices*.)

Hallucinations are actually very common: studies indicate that around 10–15 per cent of us experience them at some stage of our lives. When one nationally representative British survey asked people whether 'over the past year there have been times when you heard or saw things that other people couldn't?', 4 per cent said that they had. One per cent of interviewees reported hearing voices when there was no one else around at some point during the previous twelve months.

Hallucinations aren't only associated with periods of anxiety and stress: for example, many people describe hearing voices as they fall asleep at night or first thing in the morning as they wake up. Just like the other internal triggers we've looked at, it's the way we *try to make sense* of hallucinations that can lead to suspicious thoughts. We could see them as normal, everyday experiences. But for many of us the 'explanation' is that they are caused by the actions of *other people*.

Inebriation through drugs or alcohol

Surveys indicate that large numbers of people take 'recreational' drugs such as cannabis, ecstasy and cocaine. For some it's an enjoyable experience; others feel that any negative effects are made up for by the positive feelings the drug gives them.

Clearly drugs don't make everyone who uses them paranoid. But for some people they can make suspicious thoughts more likely to occur. Cannabis (or grass, weed, reefers, skunk, marijuana, ganja, hashish) in particular is commonly associated with feelings of paranoia. But a wide range of other drugs can also play a part in triggering suspicious thoughts:

- **Stimulants** Such as amphetamines (speed), cocaine, khat and ecstasy (and even caffeine if we drink enough of it).
- **Hallucinogens** For example, LSD (acid) and mescaline.
- **Glue and other solvents.**
- **Alcohol** When drunk regularly in large quantities.

Drugs can lead to persecutory thoughts because *they change the way we perceive the world and the way we feel inside.* They can cause *arousal, anxiety* and *anomalous experiences*. For example, we may feel detached or unreal; or we might find ourselves in a state of heightened sensitivity, even to the extent of feeling out of control. We might feel panicky or things can leap into our consciousness that seem especially significant or special. Hallucinogens (as their name suggests) can trigger hallucinations.

The range of effects that drugs can have on us is huge, but what they have in common is this alteration of our normal state. Some people find this pleasurable. For others, the changes drugs bring about feed into suspicious thoughts. When we try to *understand* these changes in the way we feel and perceive the world around us, we may see in them evidence that other people want to harm us. In most cases, these feelings disappear once the drug is out of our system, but for some people the effects can last longer. If you do get suspicious thoughts and are using drugs, you may want to consider whether the drugs are a factor.

Cannabis and paranoia

To discover whether cannabis really does cause paranoia in vulnerable individuals, we carried out the largest ever study of the effects of THC (Δ^9-tetrahydrocannabinol). THC is the main psychoactive ingredient in cannabis (meaning that it affects the way the brain functions).

We recruited 121 volunteers, all of whom had taken cannabis at least once before, and all of whom reported having experienced paranoid thoughts in the previous month (which is typical of half the population). None had been diagnosed with a mental illness. The volunteers were randomly chosen to receive an intravenous 1.5mg dose of either THC (the equivalent of a strong joint) or a placebo (saline). To track the effects of these substances, we used the most extensive form of assessment yet deployed to test paranoia, including a virtual-reality scenario, a real-life social situation, self-administered questionnaires and expert interviewer assessments.

The results were clear: THC caused paranoid thoughts. Half of those given THC experienced paranoia, compared with 30 per cent of the placebo group: that is, one in five had an increase in paranoia that was directly attributable to the THC. (Interestingly, the placebo produced extraordinary effects in certain individuals. They were convinced they were stoned, and behaved accordingly. Because at the time we didn't know who had been given the drug, we assumed they were high too.)

THC also produced other unsettling psychological effects, such as anxiety, worry, lowered mood and negative thoughts about the self. Short-term memory was impaired. And the THC sparked a range of 'anomalous experiences': sounds seemed louder than usual and colours brighter; thoughts appeared to echo in the individuals' minds; and time seemed to be distorted.

Why is cannabis such a potent trigger for paranoia? Our statistical analysis showed that in our experiment the culprits were THC's negative effects on the individual's mood and view of the self, and the anomalous sensory experiences it can produce. Negative emotions leave us feeling down and vulnerable. Worry leads us to the worst conclusions. So when we try to make sense of the anomalous experiences – when we try, in other words, to understand what's happening to us – the world can appear a weird, frightening and hostile place. Hence the paranoia. Our analysis suggests that the impairments in short-term memory did not increase the paranoia.

Clearly cannabis doesn't cause these problems for everyone. And the suspiciousness wore off as the drug left the bloodstream. But the study does show that paranoia isn't tenuously linked to THC: for a significant number of people, it's a direct result.

As you'll probably have noticed, there are many similarities between the various *internal triggers* for suspicious thoughts:

- We feel **different inside**, which can make us feel vulnerable.

- We feel **aroused**, with heightened sensitivity to the world around us. We may feel things are getting out of control.
- We have **anomalous experiences**. Sounds can seem louder and more intrusive than normal, and colours too vivid. We might feel that we, or the world around us, aren't real. And we may experience hallucinations.

When we feel like this, all sorts of things that would normally seem trivial can suddenly take on huge importance. We feel odd inside, and we notice odd things in the world around us – it can easily seem as if something is wrong. And when we try to understand what we're experiencing, we can begin to suspect that *other people are to blame.*

Medical and psychiatric conditions

Among us all, suspicious thoughts are very common. One survey suggested that 70 per cent of people have had such feelings at some point in their lives.

Paranoia, then, is something almost all of us have experienced. You could say it's normal. However, it's also associated with a number of specific medical conditions, which we'll discuss in the next couple of pages. Having suspicious thoughts doesn't mean that you have any of these conditions

– and it doesn't mean that you're going to develop them. But if you *do* have one of these medical conditions, you're much more likely to also have strong persecutory thoughts.

Psychiatric disorders

Today we know that people experiencing very common health problems, such as anxiety and depression, are much more likely to experience suspicious thoughts. But the traditional psychiatric view only really considered paranoia in the context of *psychosis*.

The term psychosis covers a number of psychiatric conditions (or mental illnesses), including **schizophrenia** and **bipolar disorder**. At present in the UK there are somewhere between half a million and a million people who have been diagnosed as suffering from psychosis.

People with these illnesses can sometimes experience very powerful paranoia. They can have strong beliefs that others don't share (known as *delusions*). They can hear voices when no one is around, and see and feel things that people around them don't see or feel (**hallucinations**). Often the voices that people hear are very critical – Cameron, the twenty-six-year-old photographer that we heard from in Chapter 1, provides a typical example of this sort of experience:

> *My ex-girlfriend's family are persecuting me. They want me to disappear. They make me hear these voices – the voices are always negative, always horrible, always putting me down.*

It's worth remembering that it's not just people diagnosed with psychosis who experience hallucinations and delusions. As we've noted, lots of us have these experiences, cope perfectly well and enjoy good mental health. It's when these experiences are so strong that they interfere significantly with our lives that people are said to have a mental illness. And for those who *are* dealing with psychosis, the ways in which it affects people are very varied. For some it's a one-off experience; for others it's an occasional occurrence; for still others it's a continuous thing.

We should bear in mind too that even among the psychological and medical professions there's a lot of debate about how helpful diagnoses like psychosis or schizophrenia really are. For one thing, recent research has suggested that schizophrenia isn't a distinct disorder, but instead a catch-all term for a number of different problems. There's a great deal of stigma attached to these conditions: it can be a very negative label for people to deal with. And there's a bigger point: how useful are these terms for psychiatric disorder when there's no real agreement on what mental illness really is? After all, it's hard to draw a clear dividing line between good mental health and mental illness. For many of us, our mental health is better at some times than others.

This isn't to say that these diagnoses are never useful. They do help us identify people who are likely to be severely affected by paranoia. And some people living with these conditions can find the diagnosis helpful – it puts a name to the experiences they've been undergoing. Also, diagnoses help medical staff decide on appropriate medication (we discuss medication in Appendix 1).

But despite the controversies concerning the nature of mental health and diagnoses such as psychosis and schizophrenia, there's lots of evidence to suggest that the approach we outline in this book – based on the ideas of cognitive behavioural therapy – can be beneficial for everyone experiencing suspicious thoughts, whether we're suffering from mental illness or not. You might remember from Chapter 1 that cognitive behavioural therapy is based on the principle that *if we can understand and change the way we think, we can change the way we feel*. A recent British Psychological Society report states:

> *There is now overwhelming evidence that psychological approaches [such as cognitive behavioural therapy] can be very helpful for people who experience psychosis . . . CBT (in this context sometimes called CBTp, short for CBT for psychosis) is a structured talking therapy which looks at the way that people understand and react to their experiences . . . The National Institute for Health and Care Excellence (NICE) considers the evidence strong enough to recommend that everyone with a diagnosis of schizophrenia should be offered CBT.*

You can find details of this report and a list of helpful books and websites at the end of this book. As we've mentioned though, cognitive behavioural therapy – and specifically the strategies for dealing with suspicious thoughts we set out in this book – can help a wide range of people. The key thing is the *distress* that our suspicious thoughts cause. If the distress is mild, you may need to do little more than read this book. If it's more pronounced, you may want to be more active in using the ideas we go on to talk about. If the distress is really troubling for you, it might be advisable to seek professional assistance to help you work through the ideas we set out (we provide some pointers to useful organisations and resources in Appendix 1).

Other medical conditions

In addition to psychiatric disorders, there are a number of other medical conditions that can trigger suspicious thoughts. If you or a relative have any of these conditions, you may find it helpful to be aware of the connection – you might, for example, want to discuss the issue with your doctor.

- **Hearing loss** Loss of hearing is common as we grow older and it can sometimes be a factor in the development of suspicious thoughts. After all, if we can't hear what's being said, we might well worry that people are talking behind our backs.
- **Dementia** Suspicious thoughts often occur in older people who are developing dementia (for example, Alzheimer's disease). Dementia makes

people confused and disorientated and means it is much harder for them to make sense of events. The suspicious thoughts often focus on the worry that the sufferer's property is going to be, or has been, stolen.

- **Alcohol and drug dependency** Earlier in this chapter we discussed the way suspicious thoughts can be triggered by drugs or alcohol. The link is even greater for people who have alcohol and drug dependency problems (often called 'addictions').
- **Epilepsy** For a small number of people this illness seems to trigger suspicious thoughts. This is particularly the case for people with temporal lobe epilepsy.

Chapter summary

- There are two main types of trigger for suspicious thoughts: the situations, events and experiences we encounter in the world and the way we feel inside. We call these **external** and **internal** triggers.
- Common external triggers are: social situations; situations from which it's difficult to escape;

unusual events; solitude; when we feel exposed; situations in which we think we might be blamed, accused, mocked or criticised.

- Common internal triggers are: our emotions; feelings of arousal; anomalous experiences; when we've taken drugs or drunk excessive alcohol.
- For both internal and external triggers, suspicious thoughts are brought about by our attempts to **make sense of ambiguous events or feelings**: we think that ***other people*** **may be to blame**.
- Suspicious thoughts are also associated with a number of medical and psychiatric conditions, though having these sorts of thoughts doesn't necessarily mean we either have one of these conditions or are about to develop it.

3

Common reactions to paranoid and suspicious thoughts

Introduction

At the beginning of this book we tried to define what suspicious thoughts are – and we also discovered that they are amazingly widespread. Almost all of us at some stage of our lives experience these sorts of worries. In Chapter 2 we described the common triggers for suspicious thoughts – the events or feelings that seem to spark these experiences. In this chapter, we look at the various ways in which people *react* to suspicious thoughts.

We begin by identifying the most common reactions. We then present the results of a survey of over a thousand people. The survey shows which of these common reactions people feel are the most helpful, and which are the least helpful. And we finish off with a questionnaire to help you analyse your own reactions to suspicious thoughts.

All of the reactions we discuss in this chapter are understandable responses to what can be quite disturbing experiences. But as we'll see, some of them are likely to make us feel better and some will probably make the problem worse. *How we react has a big impact on how well we cope with suspicious thoughts*. If you're not coping as well as you'd like, you may find that changing the way you respond to them can make a real difference. As you read through the following pages, think about the way you respond to suspicious thoughts and consider the reactions that other people find helpful.

Common reactions

The typical responses to suspicious thoughts are:

- **Ignoring** them;
- Taking a **problem-solving** approach;
- Responding **emotionally**;
- **Avoiding** them;
- Treating them as if they might be **correct**;
- Trying to **understand** them.

In a moment we'll look at each of these reactions in detail. But before we do it's worth mentioning that – as you may have found in your own case – our reactions to suspicious thoughts may involve a combination of these responses and may vary a lot, depending on the situation. Over time, too, we may find that the reactions we used to find helpful no longer work so well.

Ignoring suspicious thoughts

Emily is the thirty-four-year-old solicitor whose anxiety in social situations we heard about in the previous two chapters. We asked Emily whether she could remember a time when social events *hadn't* triggered suspicious thoughts. She told us:

> *Well, sometimes it feels like it's been this way forever! But actually I think it's something that's developed since university. Before that either I didn't have the thoughts or, when I did, they just didn't seem important. For example, I do remember being at parties when I was at university and on the odd occasion wondering whether people were laughing at me, and there was one girl I suspected might be speaking about me behind my back. But it was as if the thoughts popped into my head and popped right out again. I never spent any time worrying about them.*

It's striking that, though Emily has had suspicious thoughts for a long time, *they haven't always been a problem for her*. In fact, their effect on her used to be so insignificant that it didn't seem to matter to her whether she had them or not. Either way, they didn't have any impact. If suspicious thoughts did occur, Emily took no notice: *she ignored them.*

You might be surprised to learn that ignoring suspicious thoughts is actually the most common reaction. It might suddenly occur to us that another person is behaving suspiciously. But we don't let the thought affect us. We carry on with what we're doing and think no more about it. *We let the thought go.* Just like Emily, people often do this without making a conscious decision. If we think about the thought at all, it's only to the extent of noticing it as a thought. But we don't see it as true or important: it's just another of the thousands of thoughts we have each day, most of which – like this one – we soon forget.

Emily's reaction was spontaneous and almost unconscious. On the other hand, some people develop a deliberate strategy of ignoring their suspicious thoughts. They decide: *If people are trying to upset or provoke me, I'm not going to rise to the bait. They can say or do whatever they like, but it's water off a duck's back to me.* This is a strategy that gives the individual the sense that they are in control. They have the upper hand over the people that seem to mean them harm, which can be a hugely comforting feeling.

Remember that ignoring suspicious thoughts, consciously or unconsciously, doesn't mean that these thoughts don't occur – and it's not a question of trying to avoid them either. Suspicious thoughts happen but we simply ignore them, often without even trying. Later in this book we'll find out why many of us find it so difficult to deal like this with suspicious thoughts. That said, if we think back hard enough, we can probably remember a time when we managed to ignore a suspicious thought and get on with what we were doing.

The problem-solving approach

Rather than just ignoring suspicious thoughts, some people analyse them calmly and carefully. When we adopt this approach, *suspicious thoughts are a problem to be solved.* We try to discover why they're occurring and whether they're accurate. We look for evidence – and particularly evidence that the thoughts aren't true. We might also ask other people for advice on how to deal with them. We try to put them in context and look at the wider picture; for example, by remembering the occasions when people have been kind or supportive.

The emotional response

> *One of the worst things about the situation was the fact that, once I'd begun to worry that I wasn't wanted at work, it seemed impossible to shake off the thoughts. As they got stronger, and happened more often, I felt overwhelmed by them – it made me really miserable. I'd try to concentrate on other things but found that I couldn't. I was disgusted with myself. I felt like I should have been able to deal with the situation. I was sure other people would have handled it much better than me.*

These comments from Keith, the postal worker we've heard from several times already in this book, give us an excellent insight into the *emotional* response to suspicious thoughts. We don't ignore our suspicions, neither do we try to analyse them. Instead, we take them to heart: *they upset us*. We may feel hopeless or frustrated. Our worries seem a sign of our weakness. They dominate our lives and there seems to be nothing we can do about it. The situation is often made worse by the sense that we really *ought* to be able to cope with these sorts of thoughts.

Avoiding suspicious thoughts

Although we may feel that our suspicions aren't justified, the distress they cause can prompt us to *avoid the situations that trigger these thoughts*. In Chapter 2 we heard how Ian, an engineering student, would worry when seeing a group of people in the street:

> *I tend to deal with this by trying to hurry past them. I make sure I don't look at them in case I draw more attention to myself. If someone bumps into me, I wonder whether they did it deliberately. Rationally, I know I'm not really in danger, but that doesn't stop me worrying. At a couple of times in my life, this sort of thing has even made me a bit reluctant to go out alone, especially at night. If I had to go out, I'd try to make sure a friend was coming with me.*

Just like Ian, we may start to withdraw from the situations and people that prompt our suspicions. We may avoid talking about our feelings too: we try to pretend they don't exist. For some people, drinking or taking drugs offers a way of blotting out their worries.

Avoiding suspicious thoughts can make us feel better, but the benefit tends to be short term. In the longer run, we can find ourselves having to put a growing amount of energy into avoidance. This means a big increase in the impact that our suspicious thoughts have on our day-to-day lives. Eventually we can feel trapped by the very worries we're working so hard to avoid.

Treating suspicious thoughts as if they might be correct

Some of us react to suspicious thoughts by treating them as if they might be correct. We fear that people *really might be trying to harm us*. This tends to prompt a range of *safety behaviours* – actions we take to make it less likely that the threat will actually be carried out.

Common safety behaviours include:

- **Avoiding** the situations in which we feel threatened (in exactly the sort of way we have just discussed).
- If we can't avoid those frightening situations, we might adopt a range of other **defensive tactics** to deal with the perceived threat. For example, in Chapter 1 we mentioned Kelly, a thirty-nine-year-old mother of three, who felt that a neighbour wanted to break into her house

and steal her property. Kelly's response was to make regular checks on her door and window locks and to consider buying a burglar alarm. Similarly, we've just heard from Ian, who sometimes found that the only way he could face a trip out was by persuading a friend to come too. Other very common defensive tactics are avoiding eye contact, keeping our distance from apparent threats and looking out for possible escape routes.

- **Trying not to provoke or anger** the people we fear. For example, if we're worried about our neighbours, we might try to make as little noise as possible so as not to disturb them. Alice, the lecturer we heard about earlier in this book, sought to avoid provoking the colleagues she thought were plotting to have her fired by being as friendly as possible at work:

  I went on a charm offensive. I laughed at everyone's jokes. I made time to chat with absolutely everyone – even people I really didn't know very well. I'd bring people presents on their birthday. I'd suggest we all went out for drinks or a meal or to the cinema. Heaven knows what people made of all this!

- A smaller number of people react in the opposite way. Instead of trying to defuse any potential conflict, they opt for aggression and angrily confront those they think want to do them harm.

- **Seeking help from others** – for example, the police or the local council. Sometimes people pray that God will intervene to save them from potential threat; for others, prayer offers emotional support when they're dealing with persecutory thoughts.
- **Worrying about the perceived threat**. In Chapter 1, we heard from Serena, who suspected that a housemate was trying to steal her possessions and even to poison her. Serena went on to tell us:

  I'd be thinking about my housemate and what she might have in mind for me all the time. It was the first thing I thought about when I woke up and the last thing in my mind when I went to sleep at night. In between, all day, I'd be worrying. It was my way of stopping anything bad happening – as if worrying was a way of keeping an eye on my housemate.

For many of us, worrying is a form of **vigilance**. If we let our guard down for a moment by thinking about something else, we feel as though we'll be risking the very harm we're trying so hard to avoid.

Trying to understand suspicious thoughts

This is a reaction you're probably familiar with – after all, you're reading this book!

The most common step people take in their bid to find out more about their anxieties is simply to *talk about them with other people*. They might speak to friends or family, their doctor, or maybe a counsellor. Of course, the people we talk to might not be well placed to advise us on the best ways of dealing with these sorts of worries. But even so, talking to other people about our concerns is almost always worth the trouble. At the very least, we get another viewpoint on our ideas. If we're lucky, we may also get some reassurance and advice.

There's often another benefit too. The effort involved in explaining our fears to another person can mean that we're expressing those anxieties more fully than we've done before. We also get to hear them out loud. Instead of a jumble of thoughts rattling around our brain, we're presented with some clearer statements of the problem. All this helps give us perspective on our worries and makes it a little easier for us to assess whether they're justified or not.

Ten of the best (and ten of the worst)

We asked more than a thousand people to identify the most effective strategies for coping with suspicious thoughts. Here's the top ten:

1. Don't see the problem or situation as a threat.
2. See the situation for what it is and nothing more.
3. Try to find the positive side to the situation.
4. Have presence of mind when dealing with the problem or situation.
5. Feel completely clear-headed about the whole thing.
6. Be realistic in your approach to the situation.
7. See the problem as something separate from yourself so you can deal with it.
8. Keep reminding yourself of the good things about yourself.
9. Get things into proportion – nothing is really that important.
10. Just don't take things personally.

Several of these responses emphasise the importance of *not exaggerating the threat* in any situation. Don't give your suspicious thoughts more attention than they deserve. Instead, try to assess them calmly and realistically. If we think back for a second to the common reactions we discussed in the first part of this chapter, we can see that the top ten are generally examples of either *ignoring* suspicious thoughts, or taking a *problem-solving* approach. What also emerges is the benefit we can gain from *staying positive about ourselves*. Don't let suspicious thoughts knock your self-confidence. Don't allow them to stop you doing the things you like to do. Remember that there *are* people who like and respect you.

Although it doesn't get a mention in the top ten, one other coping strategy stood out from the results of our survey. The people who were most willing to *talk about* their feelings were also the people least likely to be troubled by suspicious thoughts. It's another reminder of the benefits of sharing our worries with other people.

Of course the kinds of strategies we've talked about here aren't always easy to put into practice. But *they can be learned* – and this book will help you to learn them.

You may be wondering which reactions to suspicious thoughts were rated the *least helpful* in our survey. Here's the list:

1. Becoming lonely or isolated.
2. Feeling that no one understands.
3. Feeling worthless and unimportant.
4. Becoming miserable or depressed.
5. Feeling helpless – as if there's nothing you can do about the situation.
6. Criticising or blaming yourself.
7. Avoiding family or friends.
8. Feeling overpowered and at the mercy of the situation.
9. Stopping doing hobbies or following interests.
10. Daydreaming about times in the past when things were better.

What stands out very clearly in these reactions is how *emotional* they are. Instead of ignoring our suspicious thoughts or seeing them as a problem to be solved, we feel miserable, worthless, overwhelmed. And when we feel like this, we inevitably cut ourselves off from our family and friends, perhaps in a bid to *avoid* the situations that seem to spark our anxieties. Hobbies no longer interest us. Our world shrinks until it seems that there's only room for our fears.

When we react like this we may wonder whether our suspicious thoughts are actually a sign that we're losing the plot – it can seem as if we're going mad. But, as we've mentioned earlier, nearly everyone has suspicious thoughts. If having these feelings is a sign of madness then pretty much all of us are in the same boat! So, having suspicious thoughts doesn't mean we're going mad. Far from being an indication of madness, our suspicious thoughts are the *understandable* products of the lives we lead and the experiences we've had. In Chapters 4 and 5, we'll look in detail at how suspicious thoughts arise and persist.

Of course, though suspicious thoughts aren't a sign of madness, they can certainly cause considerable distress. For a minority of people, these experiences can make them clinically depressed and anxious. And, as we discussed in Chapter 2, suspicious thoughts can sometimes be associated with psychosis, a psychiatric illness. In these cases, professional help may be essential. If you or a loved one are affected in this way, you may find the information given in Appendix 1 particularly helpful.

But these levels of distress are by no means common or inevitable. For the great majority of people, it's perfectly possible to gain control over suspicious thoughts without seeking professional help. And showing you how is what this book is all about.

How do you react to suspicious thoughts?

How do you react to suspicious thoughts? The exercise below will give you an indication of your typical responses.

First, think back to a time over the past month when you had a suspicious thought. Tick the box that best describes your reaction. Try to remember how you felt at the *exact moment* that the thought came to you, rather than how you reacted later. Once you've done this, repeat the exercise for three other times that you've experienced suspicious thoughts.

After you've completed the exercise, ask yourself the following questions:

- *Is this how I'd like to react?*
- *Could I have reacted in other ways?*
- *What other reactions would have been better for me?*

You're only a little way through this book, and we've only just begun to outline some positive ways in which you can deal with your suspicious thoughts. But, early as it is, are there any changes you think you could make *now* when you have a suspicious thought? For example, could you listen to them less or take a more analytical approach?

Exercise: How do you react to suspicious thoughts?

Ignoring suspicious thoughts

- I ignored the thought. ❑
- I hardly noticed the thought. ❑
- I felt quite detached from the thought. ❑
- It didn't really seem to matter. ❑
- I felt a bit anxious when the thought occurred, but I just got on with what I was doing. ❑

The problem-solving approach

- I considered the thought and rejected it. ❑
- I didn't panic and instead I thought it all through carefully. ❑
- I thought of all the reasons why the thought couldn't be correct. ❑
- I wondered what advice my friends would give me. ❑
- I put the thought into context and instead concentrated on positive things. ❑
- I decided to see what someone else thought about my anxious feeling. ❑

The emotional response

- I felt miserable. ❑
- I felt overwhelmed. ❑
- I was annoyed at myself. ❑

It felt like things were out of control. ❑

I felt vulnerable and helpless. ❑

I felt ashamed. ❑

Avoiding suspicious thoughts

I wanted to withdraw from everybody. ❑

I knew that I had to get away from the situation in order to stop the thoughts occurring. ❑

I didn't want anyone else to know I'd had the thought. ❑

I knew the only way I was going to feel better was by avoiding the thought. ❑

I thought that the only way to cope was to have a drink or a smoke. ❑

Treating suspicious thoughts as if they might be correct

I believed the thought was probably true and so I needed to get away from the situation. ❑

I tried to watch out for the danger. ❑

I tried to escape the danger. ❑

I was anxious and wanted to get somewhere safe. ❑

I wanted to blend in and not upset anyone. ❑

I got angry with the people involved. ❑

I worried about what was going to happen. ❑

I vowed to avoid these situations in future. ❑

Trying to understand suspicious thoughts

I knew I had to get more information before deciding what to do. ❑

I thought it was better to be uncertain about what was going on than leap to conclusions. ❑

I didn't know what to think but I knew I had to find out more. ❑

I wanted to talk about it with other people to check whether I was being reasonable. ❑

Chapter summary

- How we react to suspicious thoughts has a big impact on how well we cope with them.
- Common reactions to suspicious thoughts are to ignore them; to treat them as a problem to be solved; to respond emotionally; to avoid them; to treat them as if they might be correct; to try to understand them.
- The most helpful responses to suspicious thoughts involve keeping them in perspective, talking them over and not letting them disrupt our lives.
- The least helpful reaction is the emotional response. The thoughts make us miserable and can lead to us withdrawing from normal life.

4

Understanding why paranoid and suspicious thoughts occur

CASE STUDY 1: EMILY'S STORY

My name is Emily. I'm thirty-four years old. I was brought up in north London, where I live now. I work as a solicitor. I'm married and have a two-year-old daughter.

For quite a while now I've been finding social situations pretty difficult. Sometimes I worry that people are talking about me or laughing at me. Sometimes I find myself feeling very distant from the people I'm with – as if I don't belong. From time to time I've felt as if I weren't there at all – like I've somehow vanished. It's been troubling me for a long time, but it seems to have got much worse over the last couple of years. I'm at the stage now where I find myself turning down invitations. Staying at home seems a much less stressful option.

I first started having these thoughts just after I left university. Actually, that's probably not quite right. I do remember being at parties when I was at university and on the odd accasion wondering whether people were laughing at me, and there was one girl I suspected might be speaking about me behind my back. But it was as if the thoughts popped into my head and popped right out again. I never spent any time worrying about them, I really didn't. I can't imagine how I managed it, but I did.

Anyhow, after I'd finished my law studies (I had to do a degree and then another course after that, all of which was really hard), I worked as a trainee solicitor for two years at a law firm in Manchester. I found that period quite tough. I'd built up a lot of debt during my studies – I think most students do. I was getting a salary, but it wasn't much. I found the work really exhausting – I was used as a dogsbody, given all the chores no one else wanted to do. I worked really long hours. Plus, I was convinced I'd made a big mistake in moving north. I didn't know anyone else in the city. Family and friends seemed a very long way away. I made friends eventually but I'm not sure I ever really felt at home.

My memories of that period are dominated by two feelings: exhaustion and misery! I really worried that I'd made the wrong decision taking up law and several times I strongly considered giving it up. I think there were two reasons why I didn't. First, I didn't want to disappoint my parents: they'd always been proud as punch to think that their daughter was going to be a lawyer. The other reason was that I couldn't think of anything else I wanted to do. Neither of these now seem very good reasons for keeping going! I've been a solicitor for ten years, but even now I wonder whether it's the right job for me. The hours can be long and don't combine well with family life. The work can also be a strange mixture of the boring and the stressful. There are lots of good bits, of course, but I'm still on the lookout for that perfect job. Maybe I'll find it before I retire!

It was during my time in Manchester that I first noticed that I was maybe becoming a little paranoid. The firm that I worked for was a large one – lots of lawyers and lots of social events designed, I think, to test you in subtle, non-legal scenarios (or perhaps that's just my paranoid reading of it!). I found these social events pretty difficult – I dreaded them, to be honest – and as soon as one was announced I'd start worrying about it. I felt sure I was being judged. I'd see people chatting and I'd wonder whether they were talking about me. If even one person in the group happened to glance in my direction, that was it: I was sure it was me they were discussing. And if all that was followed by someone laughing – well, that was just awful. I always left as soon as I could and then I'd lie awake replaying the evening in my head. I think that at one level I knew I was being stupid – that I was imagining things. And it was funny because I'd always thought of my dad as being a bit paranoid. He was always fretting about what other people thought of us, always thinking that someone at work had it in for him. And I could see that his worries had much more to do with what was going on inside his head than what was actually going on in the real world. But knowing all this didn't make me feel any better.

Things only started to improve when I changed my job. I moved back to London and it was as if a huge weight was lifted from me – almost instantaneously! Suddenly I had a social life again. My family were nearby, plus almost all my friends from college – and lots of them from school too. And I felt far more comfortable at work. It was a much more relaxed and informal atmosphere than the company in Manchester. We used to go out a lot together after work and I never – or almost never – experienced the kind of worries that I'd had before in social situations.

Okay, so now I have to fast forward a few years! I'd almost forgotten how stressed out social situations used to make me; I hardly ever experienced the sort of paranoia I'd felt while in Manchester. But that all changed around the time my daughter was born. Actually, things were fine until I went back to work after maternity leave. I only took three months' leave because there was a lot of pressure from work. I was made to feel – though no one said so openly – that I'd be damaging my career by being away longer. So Lily went to nursery. Five days a week. I felt incredibly guilty about this. She was so tiny. I hated leaving her and I worried that I was a terrible mother for doing so. On top of this, I had all the usual pressures of work and lots of very broken nights. I don't think I've ever felt as tired as I've done over the last eighteen months, but that didn't stop me lying awake worrying about the situation.

While all this was going on, the paranoia reared its head again – and this time it was even worse than before. It got to the stage where I'd avoid going out. I was very close to quitting work. I couldn't face anyone. I knew that if someone so much as glanced at me, I'd be worrying about the meaning of that glance for days afterwards. I'd make a mental note of these sorts of 'incident' while I was out and then analyse them all when I got home, usually while lying awake in bed at night. It was crazy. I never told another soul about what I was going through. I'm not sure why. I think it was partly because I was embarrassed that so many people thought I was stupid or not up to scratch in some way. And I thought I had it all figured out: what was there to discuss? It was incredibly lonely, though. I missed the social contact; I missed my friends. And I had this awful thing, this secret, that I had to deal with all by myself. Things only changed when my husband started to doubt my repeated excuses for staying at home. He realised something was wrong – and from that point on things have got much better.

Case study 2: Keith's story

My name is Keith. I was born in Newcastle and I've never lived anywhere else. I'm not saying I've not wanted to maybe try other places, but my home is my home and I can't see myself moving now. I've worked at the Royal

Mail since I was sixteen. I'm fifty-three now, so that's thirty-seven years! I've done more or less everything in my time: delivering post, sorting mail, managing teams, managing facilities, training folk, even worked in payroll for a bit. Right now I'm back where I started: a postman. Being out and about on my own suits me at the minute.

As far as family goes, I'm currently single. I've been married twice and divorced twice. First time around, I was twenty: much too young. We split up after four years together. I married again when I was twenty-nine. Second time around was better: we were together twenty years and had three kids – all girls. I get on okay with my ex, though to be honest I don't have a lot to do with her now. I don't see as much of my kids as I'd like, but the eldest two are working down in London now so that can't be helped. Alice – she's the youngest – drops in occasionally, but she's like any teenager: her parents are the last people she wants to spend time with.

It's funny. Me and my wife both decided we'd gone as far as we could. It's not like she left me or anything. I was sad about it, of course, but I was sure it was the right thing. I was very confident I could cope. I can cook; I know how to keep house. And at first things were fine. I sorted myself out with a nice little flat and enjoyed a bit of time to myself. But it's not worked out the way I thought it would. I feel pretty cut off to tell you the truth. And the timing turned out to be bad too. First of all, I lost both my parents within a year of my divorce. My dad died of a stroke and after that my mum seemed to lose the will to live. I can understand that; they'd been together fifty years with hardly a day apart. We'd always been a very close family. I'd pop in three, four, five times a week. So them passing on was a big blow.

The other thing was that I began to have a few problems at work. I'd always been happy there, though I'm not all that great with people to be honest. I suppose I'm a bit of a loner. Not that I want to be: I just don't find it all that easy to get along with folk. I had a bit of trouble at school – bit of bullying, you know – and I don't know whether that's been a factor. Anyhow I don't mind a bit of banter – you know, a bit of leg-pulling and teasing. I can take a joke. But then my manager moved on and the guy who replaced him – well, let's just say we didn't hit it off. He was young and very cocky: thought he knew it all. To be honest, I think he saw me as a bit of a threat. Not that I wanted his job. I was very happy doing my own. But he knew I could see through him and of course he knew perfectly well that I had thirty-odd years of experience and he had about two! He also knew that I'd been through a rough time, and wasn't feeling at my best. I think he took advantage of that, to tell you the truth.

I began to notice that he was treating me differently to everyone else. He'd give me the jobs no one else wanted. He'd ignore me in meetings. If I ever wanted to see him about something, he was always busy. As you can imagine, it wound me up something rotten, but what was really infuriating was the fact that he seemed to be trying to turn my colleagues against me. I couldn't prove any of it, but I was sure that people were starting to treat me differently – people who up until then had been my mates. They'd sort of look at me oddly, or I'd walk into an office and the conversation would suddenly stop. I can think of lots of occasions when I was convinced folk were laughing at me behind my back. What before had seemed to be, you know, harmless banter now seemed like it was malicious and all aimed at me. It was as though everyone was suddenly trying to put me down. Not that I really thought through any of this. I was maybe a bit over-sensitive – as soon as something happened I didn't like, I tended to just assume the worst.

Because of this sort of thing, I suppose I withdrew into myself a bit. I found excuses for not going to the canteen at lunchtime and I didn't go to the pub after work much either. So people stopped asking me to join them, which was probably understandable but didn't make me feel any better: it just confirmed what I was already thinking. I didn't have too much else going on in my life at the time so I had plenty of opportunity to dwell on it all. It became a habit. I'd get home from work, make myself a cup of tea, and try to read the paper or have a nap. But then I'd find myself thinking back through the day. And then all kinds of things that hadn't bothered me at the time – a comment someone had made, a look I thought someone had given me – started to worry me. And I'd go on worrying about them for the rest of the night! It was like I couldn't concentrate on anything else until I'd identified all the ways in which people had tried to get at me that day. I'd be watching the TV and all of a sudden an incident I'd forgotten would come into my head and off I'd go again.

It got to the stage where I dreaded going to work. I slept badly the night before. I could feel myself tensing up on the journey in. By the time I reached the building I was in a right state: heart pounding, headache, sweating – the lot. I had to really fight the temptation to just turn around and go home. Eventually I gave in to that temptation and stayed away altogether. But that didn't help. I was disgusted with myself for giving in to these fears. I felt like I should have been able to deal with the situation. I was sure other people would have handled it much better than me. And I became a bit of a recluse. I didn't go to work and I didn't go out socialising. All day in the house on your own with no one to talk to is hard. You need a reason to get out of bed in the morning, don't you? Mine was usually to see whether anyone from work was outside in the street checking up on me. Plus I got in a stew about my next-door neighbours. I thought they were starting to look at me a bit strangely. If they were noisy at all, I used to think they were doing it to get at me. They knew I was having a hard time, so why all the banging and shouting? I don't actually think they were being particularly noisy but that's the way I was seeing things back then.

Introduction

So far in this book we've described the sorts of experiences we're referring to when we use the term 'suspicious thoughts'. We've looked at the events and feelings that can often trigger these thoughts. And we've seen how people usually react to them. But by now you might well be saying to yourself: 'All well and good, but *why* do these kinds of thoughts occur?'

You probably won't be surprised to hear that suspicious thoughts can be caused by several factors and that those factors will vary from person to person. That's the bad news for those of us hoping for a simple answer to the *why* question! The good news, though, is that there *is* an answer. We *can* make sense of our suspicious thoughts and why they occur. And once we understand our paranoia, we're a long way down the road to coping with it.

Research has identified **five main factors** involved in the occurrence of suspicious thoughts. All five are very common – all of us will have experienced at least some of them. What's important, though, is the way they combine. *Suspicious thoughts are caused by a combination of some or all of these five factors:*

- Stress and major life changes;
- Emotions (usually negative);
- Internal and external events;
- Our explanations of these internal and external events;

- Reasoning (the way we think things through and come to decisions and judgements).

In the next few pages we'll look in detail at each of these factors and show how they can combine to cause suspicious thoughts. And we'll use the stories of Emily and Keith to illustrate the model we're putting together. Of course, as we saw in Chapter 1, the content of suspicious thoughts can vary widely – for example, the type of threat we're worried about and the people we suspect of trying to harm us. But although Emily and Keith's experiences may not be identical to yours, the ideas and advice we give in the book are relevant to *all* suspicious thoughts, whatever the differences in the details. As you read the following sections, have a think about how the five factors relate to your own experiences and then complete the exercise on page 112.

The five factors

1 Stress and major life changes

For many people, suspicious thoughts seem to first appear during times of stress and change. We might, for example, be starting a new job or not be getting on with our partner. We may have suffered a bereavement or be finding it hard to make ends meet. For some people, taking drugs or drinking too much alcohol can cause stress. The stressful events can be one-offs or carry on over time. What each individual finds difficult is very much a personal thing, of course. However, the stressful experiences that form the background to the development of paranoia often seem to *involve other people*.

Stress – often caused by major life changes – certainly appears to have played a big part in the histories of both Emily and Keith. Emily's first problems with suspicious thoughts occurred when she was a trainee solicitor. She found it hard to get along with colleagues and had few friends locally. She was also suffering under the weight of family expectations: she felt that she *had* to continue with her career, despite all her misgivings, because she didn't want to disappoint her parents. We can see here how many of the stresses affecting Emily involved other people. Added to this for Emily were the pressures of starting a new job and moving to a new city – all of which she had to face on very little sleep and not enough money. No wonder, you might be thinking, she had problems!

It's striking that Emily's suspicious thoughts disappeared as soon as she took herself out of this clearly very difficult situation. They returned, though, at another time of stress and major life change. This time around the trigger seems to have been becoming a mother. Becoming a parent for the first time is an exhausting and stressful experience for many people. Added to this for Emily was the struggle to combine work and childcare. Sleeplessness was a major factor again (there's now a lot of evidence that poor sleep and suspiciousness are linked), and it's also noticeable that the pressure of other people's expectations was once more an issue. Emily came back to work sooner than she'd have liked after maternity leave, driven by worry that her company would punish her for staying away longer.

The roots of Keith's paranoid feelings also lie in a period of great stress. In his case, he had to deal with the break-up of his marriage and the isolation it seems to have brought. The death of his parents followed soon after. These huge life events can hardly have helped Keith deal with the additional challenge of having a new (and perhaps not very likeable) boss.

Stress, then, is the first of the five factors that cause suspicious thoughts. We can illustrate the way these factors combine by means of a simple diagram that we'll build up over the following sections. Here's the first part of the diagram:

Stress and major life changes
Stressful experiences, e.g. relationship problems, financial pressures, sleeplessness or shyness.
Major life changes, such as leaving home or bereavement.

↓

2 Emotions

The sorts of stresses and life changes we've just discussed often *lead to changes in the way we feel.* They can have a big effect on our emotional state – and really it would be surprising if they didn't. It's inevitable that the death of a friend or relative, or money troubles, or problems at work are going to have a major impact on our feelings. More often than not, of course, that effect is a negative one. We feel anxious or depressed. We might become unusually irritable or bad-tempered. We may develop a low opinion of ourselves or others (and sometimes both).

Our emotional state can play a big role in the development of suspicious thoughts. This is because *the way we feel has a major influence on the way we think*. Our emotions affect the way we see ourselves and others. When we're happy, we're likely to take a positive view of the world. On the other hand, feeling down is probably going to make us think negatively about things.

Of all our emotions **anxiety** is often very closely linked to the occurrence of suspicious thoughts. That connection isn't surprising. Research has shown that anxiety and suspicious thoughts are actually quite similar. In fact, *suspicious thoughts can be understood as a type of anxiety*.

Let's look at this in a little more detail. Anxiety is all about *the anticipation of threat*. It's designed to let us know when we might be in danger. Anxiety is our early warning system. It tells us that we need to take action. To use a term we discussed in Chapter 2, anxiety makes us *aroused*.

Anxiety can be a life-saver, but it can also mislead us. Many of us feel anxious even when there is no real threat. Some people become anxious at the thought of heights or enclosed spaces. Others worry when they see a dog headed their way, or if they have to take a trip in a plane. It's easy to dismiss these anxieties as irrational phobias, but they have their roots in a perfectly sensible awareness of possible danger – after all, falling from a great height is likely to kill you and enclosed spaces can be difficult to get out of. Dogs do very occasionally attack people and from time to time planes do crash. But the truth is that none of these things is very likely. Our anxiety seems *out of proportion* to the reality of the situation.

Anxiety tends to breed more anxiety. When we're anxious, we often overestimate the chances of bad things happening to us. We see danger in situations that are actually very safe. Images of the harm we fear may pop into our mind. We look inwards rather than outwards. We focus on the way we're *feeling,* rather than making a calm assessment of the world around us.

When we are anxious we tend to worry. *What bad thing is going to happen to us? How will it affect us? What can we do to prevent it?* The latest research shows that worry is a predictor of paranoid thinking. If we worry a lot we're more likely to experience suspicious thoughts. And that's no coincidence: worry fills our mind with unrealistic ideas, keeps them there, and fuels feelings of unhappiness and distress. It sounds a lot like paranoia, doesn't it?

Anxiety, then, can lead us to worry about the threat from *other people.* We view their behaviour as a danger, and – looking inwards rather than outwards – we worry about our suspicions.

Anxiety certainly seems to have played a part in the development of Emily and Keith's suspicious thoughts.

Emily's first experience of paranoid thoughts was tied up with worries about her career choice and with real anxiety about attending social events organised by her employer. When her suspicious thoughts returned, it was at a time when Emily was finding it very hard to combine the roles of mother and fulltime lawyer – and was spending lots of time worrying about her situation. In Keith's case, the thought of going to work made him so anxious that it was all he could do to stop himself turning around and heading back home.

But anxiety isn't the only emotion that can lead to suspicious thoughts:

- When we're **sad or depressed or just generally low**, we can feel particularly **vulnerable**, perhaps because we feel different or inferior to other people. Something like this seems to have been a factor in Keith's suspicious thoughts. Divorce and the death of his parents had left him feeling very low and very isolated. And the fact that Keith had been bullied at school and had felt a bit of an outsider throughout his life made him feel especially vulnerable. Keith believed his new manager took advantage of his emotional state to treat him badly and to turn his colleagues against him.
- When we're feeling low, we may also feel **guilty or ashamed**. It can seem as if the way things are going for us is actually some sort of

punishment. We might also believe that other people can see our guilt or shame and will treat us accordingly.

- **Being treated badly by people in the past** can have a lasting effect on the way we feel. This in turn can lead to us thinking that *everyone* is likely to be hostile towards us.
- When we're **angry or irritable**, it can seem as if other people are deliberately trying to provoke us. We might well blame others for whatever it is that's making us angry. When we feel like this, we tend to be very suspicious about what other people might be up to.
- For a small number of people, it's not negative emotions (unhappiness, anxiety, anger) that lead to suspicious thoughts. Rather, it's feelings of great **happiness**. We feel great about ourselves and wonder why other people don't seem to share our opinion. It can seem as if we haven't had the recognition or rewards we deserve and we may suspect that this is because of the hostile actions of other people.

Our emotions can change constantly, of course. Whatever stresses and strains we may be under, we're not necessarily anxious or depressed or irritable all the time. In the same way, suspicious thoughts may come and go.

That said, it's clear that *our emotional state plays a significant part in the development of suspicious thoughts.* The difficult situations that all of us have to deal with at some point in our lives can lead to feelings of anxiety, depression, anger and guilt. When we feel like this, we can find ourselves worrying that other people are out to harm us.

Let's build this second factor into the diagram we began on page 97:

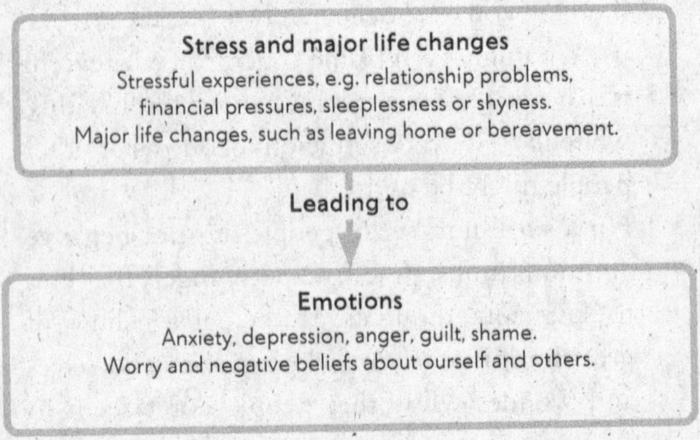

Stress and major life changes
Stressful experiences, e.g. relationship problems, financial pressures, sleeplessness or shyness.
Major life changes, such as leaving home or bereavement.

Leading to

Emotions
Anxiety, depression, anger, guilt, shame.
Worry and negative beliefs about ourself and others.

3 Internal and external events

In Chapter 2 we saw how suspicious thoughts are often triggered by the situations we encounter in the world and by the way we feel inside. We call these *external* and *internal* triggers.

Common **external triggers** are:

- Social situations;
- Situations from which it's difficult to escape;
- Unusual events, coincidences and apparent connections;
- Being alone;
- Feeling exposed;
- Situations in which we think we might be blamed, accused, mocked or criticised;
- Ambiguous verbal and non-verbal signs.

Common **internal triggers** are:

- Our emotions;
- Feelings of arousal;
- Changes in the way we perceive the world (we call these **anomalous experiences**);
- Taking drugs or drinking excessive amounts of alcohol.

These experiences form the third factor in the development of suspicious thoughts – and they're hugely important. Suspicious thoughts don't spring from nowhere. They're the result of our attempts to make sense of the way we feel and the things that happen to us. Often these events and feelings can seem very ambiguous: it's hard to know exactly what's going on. As well as being ambiguous, they can often also be pretty negative (enjoyable experiences don't seem as likely to lead to a paranoid interpretation).

In Emily's case, her suspicious thoughts were triggered the first time around by social situations at work and later by almost any form of contact with other people. She'd spend hours analysing all the ambiguous verbal and non-verbal signs she'd encountered: for example, glances and comments and smiles. And, as we saw in the previous section, Emily was also dealing with feelings of anxiety, unhappiness and guilt – all typical internal triggers. To these, we can add the fact that she was badly down on her sleep, caused the first time around by overwork and then later by overwork combined with the night-time habits of a small baby! Not getting enough sleep is a common cause of the sort of altered perception of the world we call anomalous experiences. One form Emily's anomalous experiences took was **depersonalisation** – the feeling that we don't really exist. Emily would feel this way sometimes at parties.

For Keith too there were strong internal and external triggers for his paranoid thoughts. We know that the death of his parents, and the break-up of his marriage, had left him feeling very down. We've also seen how anxious the thought of work eventually made him. His anxiety put him in a state of **arousal**, which is the term we use to describe a state of heightened sensitivity to the world around us and in particular to its possible dangers. Added to these internal triggers was the external one of simply going to work, something that for years had been straightforward for him but now with a change of manager had become extremely stressful.

One possible trigger that we haven't yet mentioned is our family background. Emily describes her father's suspicious thoughts and sees her own behaviour as very similar to his. Can our *genes* make us more or less likely to experience suspicious thoughts? The latest research suggests that they may be a factor. But our upbringing can be just as influential. Certainly we all learn ways of thinking and acting from our parents and other close family members. If they see other people as a source of danger, if they are generally mistrustful, then it's very possible that we will pick up this behaviour from them.

Our diagram of the five factors producing suspicious thoughts is taking shape. The pattern is generally this: stress leads to changes in our emotions, often making us anxious or worried or depressed. When we feel like this, we take much more notice of the way we feel and the situations we encounter. Sometimes these internal and external events are the **product** of our changed emotional state.

4 Our explanations of internal and external events

If the internal and external events we've outlined above are the third factor in the development of suspicious thoughts, the fourth is our attempt to *explain* these experiences.

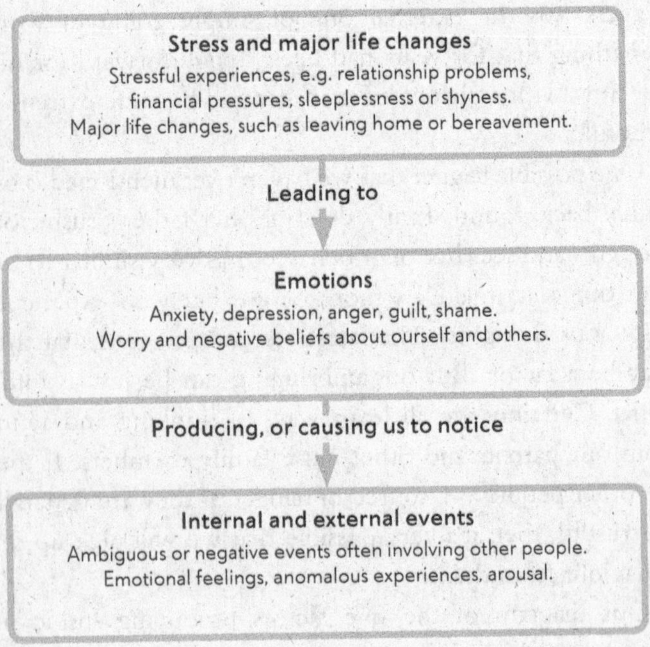

Stress and major life changes
Stressful experiences, e.g. relationship problems, financial pressures, sleeplessness or shyness.
Major life changes, such as leaving home or bereavement.

Leading to

Emotions
Anxiety, depression, anger, guilt, shame.
Worry and negative beliefs about ourself and others.

Producing, or causing us to notice

Internal and external events
Ambiguous or negative events often involving other people.
Emotional feelings, anomalous experiences, arousal.

It's perfectly natural to try to understand the world around us, and also the way we feel inside. But when we're stressed and feeling low or anxious or irritable our explanations are likely to be pretty negative. We think the worst – and often we think the worst of people around us. It can seem as if the odd or unpleasant things we've been experiencing are caused by other people. And because it's so difficult to know what anyone else is really thinking, it's all too easy to come to this conclusion. A comment from someone that wouldn't prompt a second thought when we're feeling happy can seem worryingly significant when we're stressed. We agonise for hours about what it might mean. (Of course, if there were some way to know for certain what the other person really intended we wouldn't have to endure these bouts of worry.)

Both Emily and Keith spent long periods worrying about the various external and internal events that they'd experienced (and which we've described in the preceding section).

> *I'd make a mental note of these sorts of 'incident' while I was out and then analyse them all when I got home.* (Emily)

> *I'd find myself thinking back through the day. And then all kinds of things that hadn't bothered me at the time – a comment someone had made, a look I thought someone had given me – started to worry me.* (Keith)

Both came to believe that the incidents troubling them could be explained by *the hostile actions of other people.* Instead of saying to themselves 'I'm really stressed at the moment – really uptight and upset – I need time to sort myself out', they decided they were under threat from others.

Our diagram of the five factors producing suspicious thoughts is nearly complete:

Stress and major life changes
Stressful experiences, e.g. relationship problems, financial pressures, sleeplessness or shyness.
Major life changes, such as leaving home or bereavement.

Leading to
↓

Emotions
Anxiety, depression, anger, guilt, shame.
Worry and negative beliefs about ourself and others.

Producing, or causing us to notice
↓

Internal and external events
Ambiguous or negative events often involving other people.
Emotional feelings, anomalous experiences, arousal.

Leading to
↓

Our explanation of events
Searching for understanding; worrying about what events mean.

5 Reasoning

The fifth and final part of the puzzle is **reasoning**, which is the term we use to describe the way people think things through and come to decisions and judgements.

Research has shown that it's much more likely that we'll have suspicious thoughts – and those thoughts are likely to go on for longer and cause us more distress – if we do any of the following things:

- **Thinking fast not slow** The human brain operates two basic systems for decision-making. One involves carefully considering the options and evidence. It's the kind of logical reasoning we're expected to use at school or university and, as you might expect, it can be pretty hard work! The second system is rapid, unconscious, and much more influenced by our emotions – it's the gut feeling approach to making a judgement. The Nobel prize-winning psychologist Daniel Kahnemann calls these two systems *thinking fast and slow*.

  The faster we think, the more vulnerable we are to paranoia. A decision or judgement made quickly isn't always going to be a mistake, but in general it's better to think through a situation carefully first. When we're anxious, we often rush to a decision, basing it on only a little bit of data. It's hard to take the time to think things through or gather more evidence when we're worried or afraid. But if we don't take the time to think slowly, if we don't gather and analyse the evidence for our thoughts and feelings, and if we don't talk things over with other people, we run the risk of jumping to the wrong conclusion. And that wrong conclusion may well be that other people are out to hurt us.

Emily, for example, was prone to thinking fast, and sometimes jumped to the conclusion that she was being discussed on the basis of just one piece of possible evidence: other people's glances: *If even one person in the group happened to glance in my direction, that was it: I was sure it was me they were discussing.* Emily didn't investigate any further; she didn't, for example, go over to the group to hear what they were chatting about. The same is true of Keith. He didn't take the time to think things through: *As soon as something happened I didn't like, I tended to just assume the worst.*

- **Blaming others** People usually explain events in one of three ways. Events can be caused by ourselves, by the situation or by other people. For example, if we're late for work we could blame ourselves for not getting up earlier; or we could put the blame on the congestion that can make it so difficult to get anywhere on time;

or we could blame the other commuters who pushed in front of us in the queue for a train ticket or took the last place on the bus. If we tend to see other people as the cause of events (psychologists call this *making external attributions)*, we're much more likely to have suspicious thoughts.

- **Not considering alternative explanations** Sometimes suspicious thoughts are just the first thing than comes to mind when we're thinking about experiences that we've had. But those suspicious thoughts can really take hold if we don't try to think of alternative explanations for those experiences – if we don't, in other words, focus on *thinking slow*. Emily, for example, never considered the possibility that her conclusions might have been wrong: *I thought I had it all figured out: what was there to discuss?*

  Some experiences (hallucinations, for example) can be so disturbing and so difficult to explain that it's hard to come up with alternative explanations. But we're much less likely to be troubled by suspicious thoughts if we're able to think beyond our first paranoid reaction – if we can keep in mind that what we've seen or what we feel can be explained in other ways. It might be a question of remembering that we're feeling a bit stressed or down, and reminding ourselves of the effect that can have on the way we see the world. It's these alternative explanations – these ways of seeing past our initial reaction to events – that we want to help you discover.

With this fifth factor, our model of how suspicious thoughts are caused is finally complete.

Exercise: Understanding why your suspicious thoughts occur

In this chapter we've presented the five factors that combine to cause suspicious thoughts, and we've illustrated this using a simple flow diagram. Have a go at filling in the blank diagram on page 118 using your own experiences. For each of the five factors, we've included a list of typical examples.

Stress and major life changes

- Problems with friends.
- Problems with work colleagues.
- Problems with our partner.
- Not getting on with people.
- Being bullied.
- Leaving home.

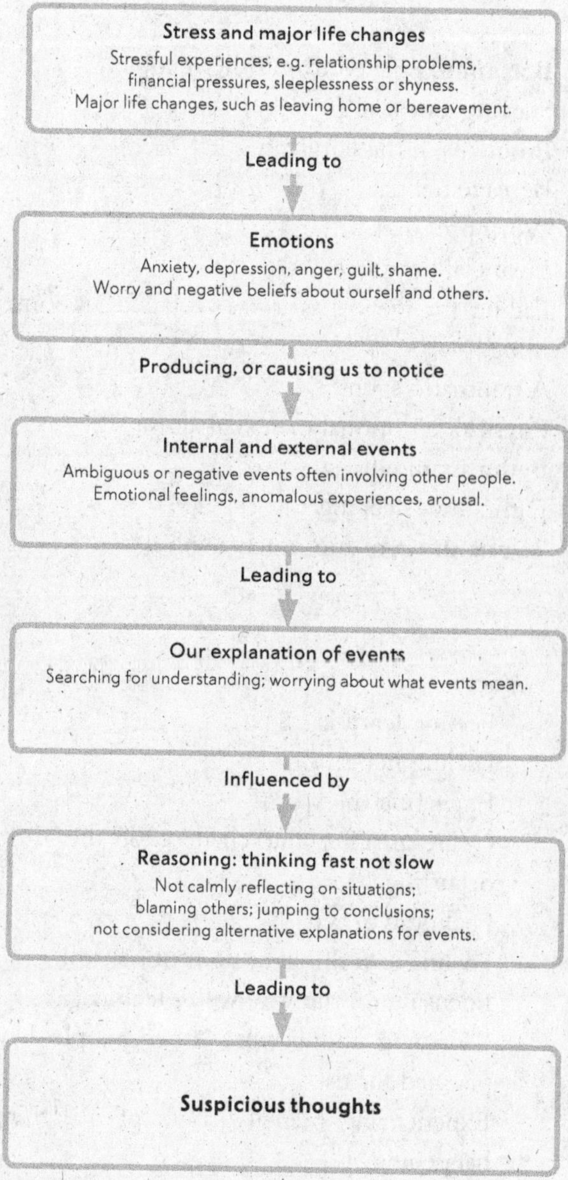

Stress and major life changes
Stressful experiences, e.g. relationship problems, financial pressures, sleeplessness or shyness. Major life changes, such as leaving home or bereavement.

↓ **Leading to**

Emotions
Anxiety, depression, anger, guilt, shame. Worry and negative beliefs about ourself and others.

↓ **Producing, or causing us to notice**

Internal and external events
Ambiguous or negative events often involving other people. Emotional feelings, anomalous experiences, arousal.

↓ **Leading to**

Our explanation of events
Searching for understanding; worrying about what events mean.

↓ **Influenced by**

Reasoning: thinking fast not slow
Not calmly reflecting on situations; blaming others; jumping to conclusions; not considering alternative explanations for events.

↓ **Leading to**

Suspicious thoughts

- Becoming isolated from other people.
- Starting a new job.
- Problems in the family.
- Bereavement.
- Work pressures.
- Financial pressures.
- Failing (or feeling as if we've failed) at something.
- A traumatic event.
- Physical, emotional or sexual abuse.
- Being assaulted.
- Difficulties sleeping.
- Taking drugs or too much alcohol.

Emotions

- Anxiety.
  - Feeling fearful.
  - Feeling nervous.
  - Expecting the worst.
  - Overestimating the chances of the threat occurring.
  - Feeling worried.
  - Feeling as if things are out of control.
  - Focusing on the way we're feeling.
  - Worrying about what other people have planned for us.
  - Experiencing mental images of bad things happening.

- Lowered mood.
  - Feeling miserable or sad.
  - Feeling vulnerable.
  - Feeling as if we're different to other people.
  - Feeling guilty.
  - Feeling ashamed.
  - Believing that we deserve to be harmed.
  - Believing that we're powerless.
  - Feeling frightened of rejection by others.
  - Dwelling on things.
- Anger.
  - Feeling angry or irritable.
  - Feeling tense.
  - Feeling as if we're on a short fuse.
  - Resenting other people.
  - Worrying about what other people might be doing to us.
- Elation.
  - Feeling overjoyed.
  - Feeling as if we're special.
  - Believing we're exceptionally talented.
  - Feeling our thoughts race.

Internal and external events

- Non-verbal signs.
  - Facial expressions.
  - The look in people's eyes.

    - Hand gestures.
    - Laughter and smiles.
    - Whistling and shouting.
- Verbal signs.
    - Snatches of conversation.
- Coincidences.
- Feeling aroused.
- Feeling that things are unusually significant.
- Anomalous experiences.
    - Things appear brighter or more vivid.
    - Sounds seem louder and more intrusive.
    - Being unusually sensitive to smells.
    - Objects seem odd to the touch.
    - Feeling as if we're not really there, or that other people aren't really there.
- Illusions and hallucinations.
- Being easily startled.
- Having trouble concentrating.

Our explanation of events

- Wanting to make sense of events.
- Trying to figure things out.
- Worrying about what's going on.
- Dwelling on things.

Reasoning: thinking fast not slow

- Relying on gut feelings.

- Not carefully reflecting on our thoughts.
- Jumping to conclusions.
- Tending to see events as caused by other people.
- Not discussing our thoughts and feelings with others.
- Not weighing up the evidence for our worries.
- Not considering that we might be mistaken.
- Not considering alternative explanations for our experiences.

Chapter summary

- There's no single reason why we experience suspicious thoughts.
- Suspicious thoughts are usually the result of a combination of five factors:
  - § Stress and major life changes.
  - § Our emotions.
  - § Internal and external events.
  - § Our interpretation of these events.
  - § Our reasoning – the way we think things through and come to decisions and judgements.

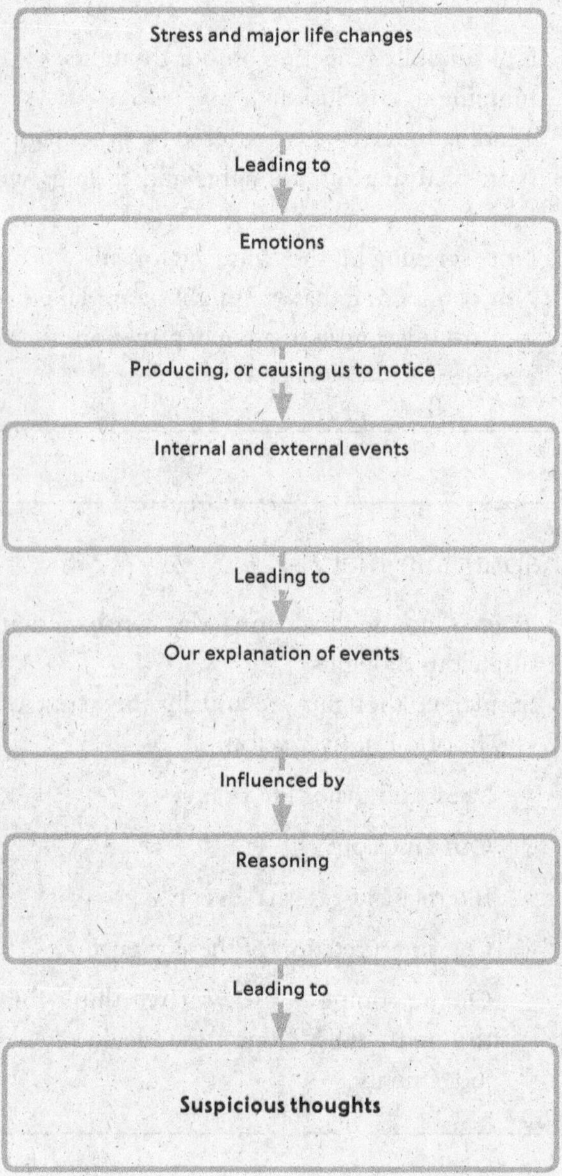

Stress and major life changes

↓ Leading to

Emotions

↓ Producing, or causing us to notice

Internal and external events

↓ Leading to

Our explanation of events

↓ Influenced by

Reasoning

↓ Leading to

Suspicious thoughts

5

Understanding why suspicious thoughts persist and why they cause distress

Introduction

As we saw in the previous chapter, suspicious thoughts are usually caused by a combination of factors. We're dealing with a stressful situation, and this has an impact on the way we feel: we might become anxious or depressed, for example. When we feel like this, we notice things that normally we'd not give a second thought to but that now seem odd or confusing. When we try to make sense of these odd events, we jump to the conclusion that other people are out to harm us.

We all have suspicious thoughts from time to time. Often we can shrug them off almost without taking any notice. Sometimes they can take hold of us and cause real problems. In this chapter, we'll show *why some suspicious thoughts keep coming back to us and why they cause us distress.* As we'll see, it's really a question of how we respond to these thoughts.

In Chapter 3 we discussed the variety of ways in which people react to suspicious thoughts: some helpful, some not so helpful. Here we're going to concentrate on four of the least helpful ones:

- Believing that our suspicions may be true;
- Behaving as if our suspicions are true;
- Feeling anxious;
- Feeling down.

Research has shown that it's these four responses that determine how long our suspicious thoughts last and how badly they affect us.

Four key responses

1 Believing that our suspicions may be true

How many thoughts do you have every day? Hundreds, certainly; thousands, quite possibly. If your thoughts are anything like ours, then most of them will come and go almost without us noticing – which may be just as well!

Out of this jumble of thoughts the ones that stand out are often emotional: we remember thinking how infuriating the noise made by our neighbours was, for example, or how happy we felt to see our friends at a party. Suspicious thoughts are also more likely to make an impression on us.

It's one thing for us to remember the suspicious thoughts that popped into our head that day, but once we start *believing* them, or thinking that they *may* be true, the following two consequences tend to follow:

- We start to notice the things that seem to confirm our suspicions and fail to notice the things that don't. Psychologists call this the **belief confirmation bias**.
- Because we believe our suspicious thoughts, we stop considering *alternative explanations* for events.

The belief confirmation bias is hardly surprising: it's very natural and very common. Almost all of us are generally more comfortable with the things we know and understand and that fit our view of the world than we are with those things that challenge our preconceptions. As long ago as the seventeenth century the philosopher Francis Bacon wrote:

> *The human understanding when it has once adopted an opinion . . . draws all things else to support and agree with it. And though there be a greater number and weight of instances to be found on the other side, yet these it either neglects and despises, or else by some distinction sets aside and rejects.*

We can see the belief confirmation bias at work in the experiences of both Emily and Keith. For Emily, social situations are opportunities for other people to do her down. All she can remember about them are the apparently ambiguous glances, or comments, or smiles that she thinks are being directed at her. Social contact seems to Emily to be just a smokescreen for hostility. Friendly behaviour makes no impression at all on her. There's a very dramatic contrast between this and Emily's attitude to social occasions at happier times of her life.

In a similar way, Keith's view of his colleagues at work focuses exclusively on the ways in which he believes they're getting at him. And something very interesting happens. Keith's suspicions influence his thinking so much that behaviour he used to find innocuous now seems quite the opposite:

> *What before had seemed to be, you know, harmless banter now seemed like it was malicious and all aimed at me.*

The drive to find incidents that confirm Keith's suspicious thoughts is so strong that it completely changes his reaction to the world around him.

Just like Emily and Keith, when we start to believe our suspicious thoughts we notice all the things that seem to confirm our fears – and none of the things that don't. We're so determined to find the evidence to prove our suspicions are correct that we put the worst possible interpretation on events. If we do come across friendly behaviour, we're likely to dismiss or distrust it rather than doubt our suspicious thoughts. So, for example, the banter at the office becomes for Keith a joke at his expense – when not long before he'd found it enjoyable. In a similar way, we might interpret a friendly gesture from a neighbour, friend or family member we're suspicious about as just a way to get us off our guard.

You won't be surprised to learn that the belief confirmation bias can be the start of a vicious cycle: the more evidence we think we've found for our suspicions, the more we believe them. The more we believe our suspicious thoughts, the less likely it is that we'll take seriously – or even notice – anything that seems to disprove them.

In a very similar way, the more we believe that our suspicious thoughts might be true, the less likely we are to consider **alternative explanations** for the events that are worrying us. As we've seen in previous chapters, it's often difficult to know for certain what people really mean by a comment or an action. Say, for example, that you pass someone you know from work in the street. You smile at them but they don't smile back. In fact, they don't acknowledge you at all. There are lots of possible explanations for this behaviour:

- They didn't see you because they weren't wearing their glasses.
- They were lost in their own thoughts.

- They're not good at recognising people out of context. They'd have noticed you at work, because that's where they'd expect to meet you.
- They ignored you because they don't like you.
- They're shy in social situations and try to avoid them.

Any of these scenarios could be true, of course – and there are probably many more possibilities. But if we're feeling suspicious, we're likely to focus on only one explanation: we assume our colleague ignored us deliberately because she doesn't like us.

Emily and Keith spend lots of time worrying about other people's behaviour, but neither of them is able to see beyond their suspicions. For Emily, the situation is straightforward: her colleagues are out to do her down (*I thought I had it all figured out*). Keith too is absorbed in his anxieties:

> *It was like I couldn't concentrate on anything else until I'd identified all the ways in which people had tried to get at me that day.*

Neither Keith nor Emily seriously considers that the behaviour worrying them so much could be explained in lots of different ways – most of which aren't troubling at all. Emily, for example, would see a group of people chatting at a social function. If one of them happened to glance in her direction, she would decide that they were talking about her. Well, that's a possible explanation for what was going on, but there are plenty of other possibilities. The group may have been discussing someone or something entirely different. If by some chance Emily was the topic of conversation, the comments might have been positive – perhaps someone was saying how impressed they'd been with her work. The person glancing in Emily's direction may have been looking at someone else, or just looking around the room. They may not even have spotted Emily. If they did see her, their feelings towards her may have been friendly. Perhaps they would have liked her to join the conversation.

You can doubtless imagine other possible explanations. What's so striking is that Emily doesn't seem to consider any of them. She thinks fast when she needs to think slow. Her suspicious thoughts are so powerful that *she focuses only on the explanation that confirms her fears*.

2 Behaving as if our suspicions are true

As you might expect, once we start *thinking* there's some truth in our suspicions, we start *behaving* differently too. Here are three common ways in which we change the way we behave:

- We adopt safety behaviours.
- We act differently when we're with other people.
- We don't try to sort out difficult relationships.

One of the most common reactions to suspicious thoughts is to adopt **safety behaviours**. As we saw in Chapter 3, safety behaviours are actions we take to make it less likely that the threat we fear will actually be carried out. The most common type of safety behaviour is staying clear of the situations in which we feel threatened – psychologists call this **avoidance**. For example, if we're worried about being attacked we might avoid going outside or to particular parts of town. But there are other types of safety behaviours. We might, for example, only go into a situation we feel is threatening with somebody we trust. We may try to please the people we think are out to get us (we call this **appeasement**). Or we might try to protect ourselves by keeping constantly on our guard.

It's perfectly natural to try to avoid danger. But one of the consequences of safety behaviours is that it then becomes very hard to know whether we really were *in danger.* For instance, Keith felt that by staying away from work he was avoiding trouble with his boss and colleagues. He assumed that his suspicions were accurate and changed his behaviour accordingly. But by doing so he also lost the opportunity to find out whether trouble was actually going to happen. After all, he may have been pleasantly surprised.

So *safety behaviours rob us of the chance to test our fears.* And if we never get to test whether our anxieties are true, we can all too easily become locked into them. As Keith and Emily both experienced, avoiding worrying situations can all too easily lead to isolation. We tend to withdraw from social contact and become less active – both Keith and Emily eventually stopped seeing other people altogether. We end up with lots of time on our hands: time we're likely to spend dwelling on our fears.

Suspicious thoughts can also change the way we act when we're with certain people. Instead of relaxing and enjoying their company, we worry about the threat they might pose to us. Often these kinds of feelings make us seem preoccupied, nervous and withdrawn. We might seem timid or secretive. Some people, on the other hand, become angry and upset. Not surprisingly, when we feel this way we're unlikely to be good company. To other people it seems like we're just not ourselves – and of course we're not: our normal self is buried beneath our suspicions.

Unfortunately, as Keith's experience shows, this change in the way we act when we're with other people has negative consequences:

> *I suppose I withdrew into myself a bit – I found excuses for not going to the canteen at lunchtime and I didn't go to the pub after work much either. So people stopped asking me to join them, which was probably understandable but didn't make me feel any better: it just confirmed what I was already thinking.*

It's another vicious cycle. Our suspicions make us difficult to be around. So after a while our friends and colleagues stop trying to spend time with us. This appears to provide even more justification for our suspicions: it seems as if people really don't like us . . .

We saw in Chapter 4 how suspicious thoughts are often rooted in stressful experiences. Difficult relationships – whether it be with a partner, a family member, a friend or a colleague – are a prime example of these stressful experiences. Keith's anxieties, for example, seemed to have their roots in the break-up of his marriage, his increasingly distanced relationship with his children, and his unhappy dealings with his manager. It's hard enough at the best of times to talk openly with someone about problems in your relationship. It's even harder when you're having suspicious thoughts about that other person. Instead of starting a dialogue about the issues that need resolving, we're likely to turn inwards and brood on our worries – just as Keith did. Keith saw very little of his ex-wife and his children, and he was unwilling or unable to talk to his manager about the tension he felt between them. He became isolated, alone with his anxieties:

> *I didn't have too much else going on in my life at the time so I had plenty of opportunity to dwell on it all.*

Once again, we can see a familiar pattern emerging. Keith's stressful relationships helped produce suspicious thoughts. The suspicious thoughts made it almost impossible for Keith to have the kind of open discussions with his ex-wife or children or boss that might have improved these relationships. Instead, Keith retreated into himself, the relationships got no better, and the suspicious thoughts were reinforced. It can be a tough cycle to break out of.

3 Feeling anxious

We've seen how suspicious thoughts are caused by our emotional response to stressful experiences. Of all the emotions, anxiety is the one that seems to be most closely linked to the development of suspicious thoughts.

But anxiety isn't just an important factor in the *creation* of suspicious thoughts; it also helps determine how long those thoughts *continue* and how badly they *affect* us. Our suspicious thoughts can often be very upsetting. The feelings of threat and danger they provoke in us are so strong that they make us anxious. After all, the purpose of anxiety is specifically to alert us to possible danger. And these new feelings of anxiety only intensify our suspicious thoughts, which then in turn increase our anxiety – and so on. It's yet another vicious cycle.

Emily's experiences provide us with a revealing example of this. Her second spell of suspicious thoughts came at a time when she was struggling to balance the competing demands of parenthood and a demanding and highly pressured job. She was gripped by anxiety about her competence as a mother and as a lawyer. She worried that trying to combine work and motherhood was unfair to her daughter; and she feared that her career could be damaged if colleagues thought she was prioritising her family over her work. The suspicious thoughts she began to have about her colleagues only increased her anxiety:

> *I knew that if someone so much as glanced at me, I'd be worrying about the meaning of that glance for days afterwards.*

Emily broods on her suspicions, turning them over and over in her mind. But as we've seen already, becoming absorbed in our worries only seems to increase them. When we can't get any perspective on our anxieties, we can become locked into them: anxiety breeds anxiety. Emily's fears escalate to the point where she is unwilling to leave the house, and on the verge of quitting the job that she has worked so hard to gain and keep.

For some people, worrying can actually be a form of safety behaviour. Worrying keeps us alert and, as such, can make us feel as though we're ready to deal with the danger. We imagine that, if we stop being anxious, we'll be letting down our guard and become suddenly vulnerable. In fact, all that this sort of constant worrying achieves is to keep us focused on our suspicious thoughts. And if our suspicions are rooted in past bad experiences, worrying can revive our memories of those experiences. Sometimes we start to worry that our anxiety is a sign that we're losing control. This is called *worry about worry* and it's something Emily experienced:

> *When I thought about the effect my paranoia was having on my life, I began to wonder whether I might be going a bit mad.*

4 Feeling down

Feeling down is – just like anxiety – an emotion that can both help cause suspicious thoughts and be a major factor in keeping them going.

Suspicious thoughts can frequently make us feel sad and miserable. And the lower we feel, the longer our suspicious thoughts are likely to stick around. Here are some common ways in which our suspicions can depress us:

- We feel out of control, as if we're powerless to shake off our worries. We can even start to fear, as Emily did, that we're going mad.
- Our suspicious thoughts can awaken all kinds of negative feelings we've harboured all along about ourselves. This was the case with Emily:

  I'd worry that, because I couldn't join in with a conversation, the others would think I was stupid. I'd think: I don't belong here. I don't fit in . . . That feeling of not belonging, of being different and isolated, is actually something I've experienced at various times of my life.

- Keith's struggle to deal with his suspicious thoughts reinforced his sense of inadequacy:

  I was disgusted with myself for giving in to these fears. I felt like I should have been able to deal with the situation. I was sure other people would have handled it much better than me.

- Sometimes we can have such a low opinion of ourselves that we feel we *deserve* to be punished or harmed.

- Our negative views about the world around us can seem to be confirmed: people are cruel, life is unfair, and the world is a dangerous place.

These kinds of feelings make us all the more receptive to our suspicions. Our fears seem more convincing than ever. As a result, they're also likely to stay with us for longer.

One more very important thing can happen when we feel down: we have much less *energy* for anything other than worrying. We withdraw into ourselves, stop socialising and generally reduce our activity levels. Both Keith and Emily ended up retreating from the world:

> *I became a bit of a recluse. I didn't go to work and I didn't go out socialising.* (Keith)
>
> *It got to the stage where I'd avoid going out. I just didn't feel up to it. I was very close to quitting work. I couldn't face anyone. I think I was just exhausted.* (Emily).

But *doing less means worrying more*. With no work or hobbies or social contact, there's really nothing else to keep us busy. Think about your own experiences: when you're busy doing something (and particularly something you enjoy), do you have more or fewer suspicious thoughts? Nine times out of ten, you'll find that you'll have far fewer suspicious thoughts.

Some conclusions

We've seen that the way we respond to our suspicious thoughts helps determine how long those thoughts stick around and how much distress they cause us. The more we do any of the following, the more prolonged and severe our experience is likely to be:

- Believe that our suspicions may be true.
- Behave as if our suspicions are true.
- Feel anxious.
- Feel down.

We can represent these four key responses and their relationship to suspicious thoughts in the following diagram.

The way our suspicious thoughts affect us is often self-perpetuating, as we've seen in the pages above. For example, they make us feel anxious, which increases our suspicious thoughts, which in turn makes us even more anxious. We've tried to show this vicious cycle in the diagram by making the arrows double-headed.

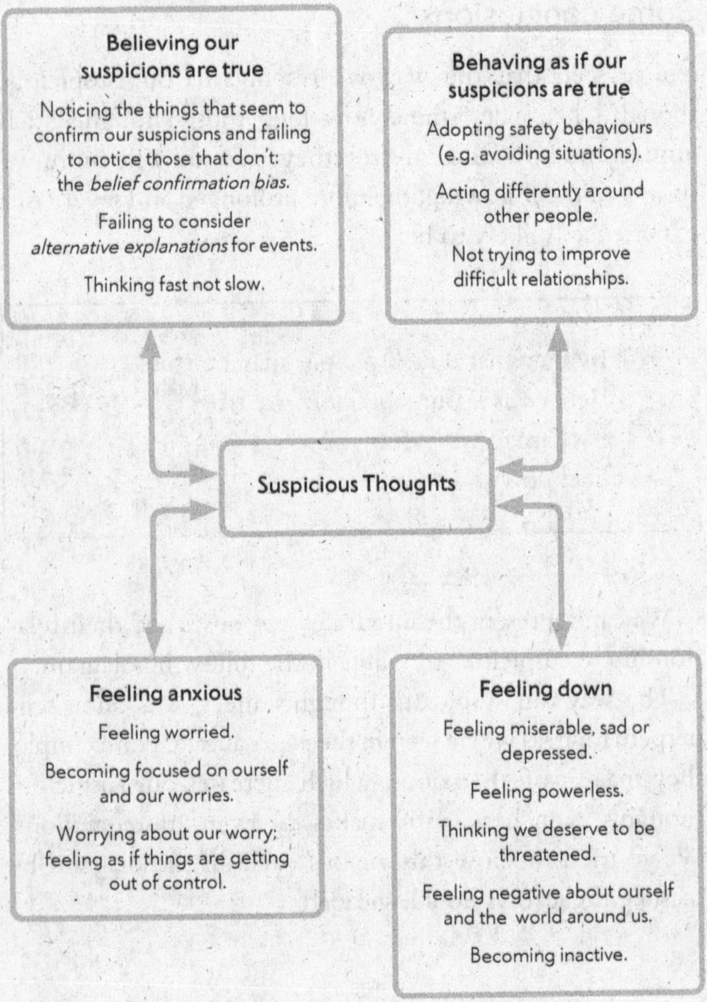

Believing our suspicions are true

Noticing the things that seem to confirm our suspicions and failing to notice those that don't: the *belief confirmation bias.*

Failing to consider *alternative explanations* for events.

Thinking fast not slow.

Behaving as if our suspicions are true

Adopting safety behaviours (e.g. avoiding situations).

Acting differently around other people.

Not trying to improve difficult relationships.

Suspicious Thoughts

Feeling anxious

Feeling worried.

Becoming focused on ourself and our worries.

Worrying about our worry: feeling as if things are getting out of control.

Feeling down

Feeling miserable, sad or depressed.

Feeling powerless.

Thinking we deserve to be threatened.

Feeling negative about ourself and the world around us.

Becoming inactive.

Exercise: Understanding why your suspicious thoughts keep coming back to you and why they cause distress

Have a look at the exercise on page 137 and fill in the diagram using your own experiences. To get you thinking, we've provided some examples of common responses.

Believing our suspicions are true

- I'm good at noticing things that seem to support my suspicious thoughts.
- I'm not good at noticing things that seem to contradict my suspicious thoughts.
- I always jump to a negative interpretation of events.
- I'm not good at thinking through the range of possible explanations for an event.
- I tend to think fast.

Behaving as if our suspicions are true

- I try to avoid situations in which I feel threatened.
- I try to get away from difficult situations.
- I tend to spend less time out with other people.
- I avoid eye contact with people.
- I keep near the exits when I am out.
- I check for potential sources of danger.
- I often look to other people for protection.
- I often think I've only managed to avoid a threatening situation by the skin of my teeth.
- I prefer being on my own.

- I'm often irritable with people.
- I'm quite secretive.
- I find it hard to have a relaxed conversation with someone.
- If I have a problem with someone, I don't feel comfortable trying to talk it through with them.

Feeling anxious

- My suspicious thoughts make me anxious.
- I spend a lot of time worrying about things.
- I try to always be prepared for danger.
- Most of the time I'm thinking about myself and my worries.
- Sometimes it seems as if my suspicious thoughts are getting out of control.
- Bad memories keep coming to mind.

Feeling down

- I generally feel quite sad.
- I often feel powerless.
- I think that I deserve to be harmed.
- I believe the world is a cruel and unfair place.
- I don't get as much enjoyment out of life as I used to.
- I do less than I used to.
- I'm a lot more passive these days – I'm more likely to spend time watching TV than going out or doing things around the house.

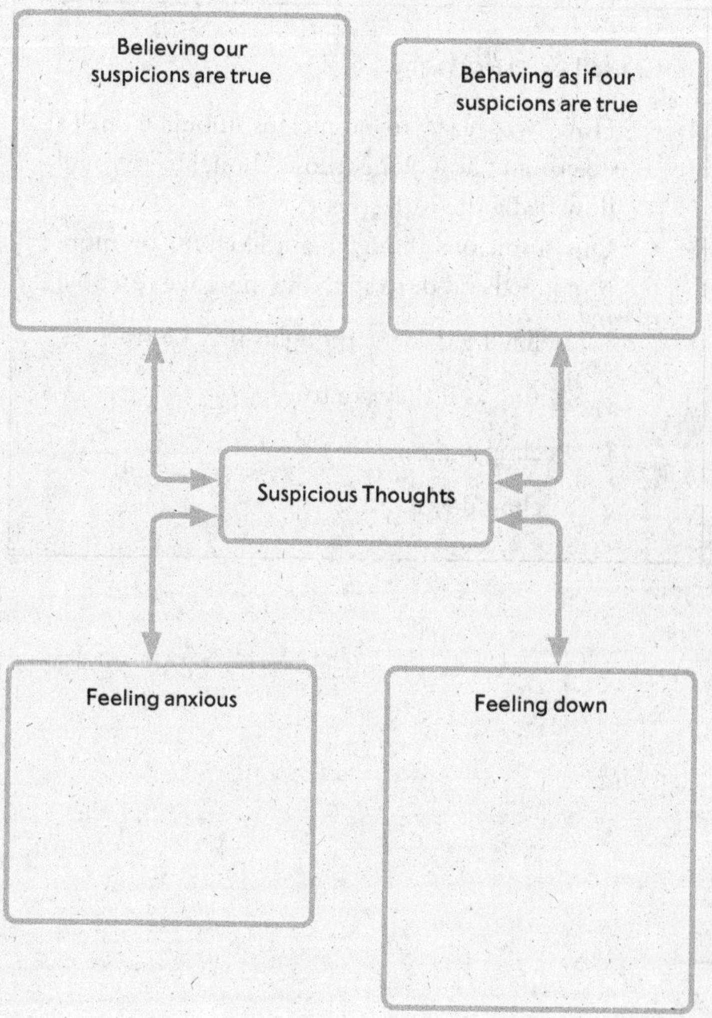
Believing our suspicions are true
Behaving as if our suspicions are true
Suspicious Thoughts
Feeling anxious
Feeling down

Chapter summary

- How we react to suspicious thoughts helps determine how long those thoughts last and how badly they affect us.
- Our suspicious thoughts are likely to be more prolonged and distressing the more we react by:

  § Believing that the thoughts may be true.

  § Acting as if they are true.

  § Feeling anxious.

  § Feeling down.

PART TWO

OVERCOMING SUSPICIOUS THOUGHTS

6

The beginnings of change

Introduction

Already you've come a long way. By sticking with us for the past five chapters, you're much further forward in your understanding of what suspicious thoughts are, why they occur and why they can cause us such problems. Over the next six chapters, we'll build on this progress with **ten practical steps** you can take to overcome your suspicious thoughts.

We can't solve a problem unless we understand it. How else would we know where to start and what to do? So the first of the practical steps (the two we cover in this chapter) are designed to help you really understand your *own* suspicious thoughts. You'll be moving on from the more general understanding of paranoia you've gained from the first half of this book to develop a detailed awareness of how and when these thoughts affect you. We want you to take a step back from your anxieties and instead become an *observer* of them.

But before we get started properly on these practical steps, let's look at some positive behaviours and attitudes that will help you succeed.

The foundations of success

> *I knew I was stronger than I've ever been, but it's what goes on in your head that counts.*
>
> Kelly Holmes

(Source: http://news.bbc.co.uk/sport1/hi/olympics_2004/athletics/3609004.stm)

None of us achieves anything unless we tackle our goals with the right attitude, and the quotation from Olympic gold medallist Kelly Holmes expresses this truth beautifully. Sports stars know that what sets champions apart is not so much their natural ability, but the mindset they adopt in order to maximise that ability. A positive mindset is the springboard for positive behaviour.

Some sports people have an instinctive feel for this mindset. But most have to learn it and then work to make it second nature. And we can all learn these good mental habits: they're useful for everyone, not just athletes. They can certainly play a big role in helping us to deal with suspicious thoughts. Remember: *it's what goes on in your head that counts*. As you work on the ten steps presented over the next chapters, see if you can adopt the following positive habits:

- Make sure you **set aside regular time** to work with this book. If we want to make progress with anything, it's so much easier if we work at it on a regular basis and not just when we happen to feel like it. We suggest you spend twenty minutes every day, or perhaps every other day, reading this book and trying out the exercises and techniques in it. It's a good idea to schedule this time in your diary – it's all too easy to let other commitments crowd out the things we want to do for ourselves. But no one likes missing an appointment – even an appointment with ourselves!
- Take it **one step at a time**. Don't rush – as the great Japanese novelist Haruki Murakami says about his own experience with writing and running, **gradually expand the limits of what you're able to do**. Stick to your guns, even if you feel like you're not making progress as fast as you'd like. You will get there in the end. Working **methodically** and **patiently** is the surest way to achieve your goals. Take it one day at a time, set small targets and gradually it will all come together.
- **Be willing to try things out.** Change is often difficult. Most of us are more comfortable with what we're used to than with new things – and especially new ideas. But just by reading this

book you've already shown that you're interested in turning things around. Try to approach the various suggestions we make with an open mind – no matter how crazy they might seem!

- **Back yourself to succeed.** Build your self-confidence by encouragement and rewards. Criticism is rarely good for motivation. Being hard on yourself will just make you feel worse. It'll put you in exactly the *wrong* frame of mind to take on any sort of challenge. So if your attempt to deal with your suspicious thoughts isn't going as well or as fast as you'd like, try not to blame yourself. Stay positive, remember the progress you've made and encourage yourself to push on to success. Reward yourself when you've completed a task. If you've tried out one of the techniques we suggest, treat yourself – buy that CD or box of chocolates. And feel good about yourself!
- **Monitor your efforts.** Sports people often watch videos of their performances so that they can get a more objective sense of their strengths and weaknesses. Videoing yourself probably isn't going to be an option, but you can still maintain a very good record of your efforts by writing them down. Keep a little notebook handy and jot down what you do from this book, what you learn and how you feel. It'll help you gain the

distance you need to think clearly about your experiences. And over time it'll also show you just how much progress you've made.

- **Set achievable goals.** One of the authors of this book (you'll have to guess which one!) likes to play tennis – but they'd also like to be a lot better at it! However, no matter how doggedly they stick to these principles, no matter how hard they try, they're never going to be able to play tennis like Roger Federer. Their game will improve, that's for sure, but never enough to win an open championship. Obviously, if our mystery tennis player has their heart set on challenging Federer, they're going to be bitterly disappointed. Despite all their efforts, their objective just isn't realistic. On the other hand, a goal to significantly improve their game is one that's well within their grasp – and one they can feel proud about achieving.

So it's really important that *we set ourselves achievable goals*. If we don't, we're just condemning ourselves to certain failure. We often meet people who desperately want never to feel paranoid again. This is completely understandable given the distress and problems that suspicious thoughts have caused them. But we always explain that what they'd like to achieve just isn't possible. And probably you'll be able to guess why we say this. It's simply because *everyone has suspicious thoughts from time to time* – just like everyone is sometimes sad or anxious. None of us can hope to be happy all the time – unhappiness is part of life. It's just the same with suspicious thoughts. Human beings are social creatures; we live surrounded by other people. It's inevitable that occasionally we'll wonder what other people are up to.

You might aim to make your suspicious thoughts occur less often. You might try to make them less upsetting. And you might want to stop them getting in the way of your social life or hobbies. All these objectives are most definitely achievable. But preventing your suspicious thoughts from *ever* occurring again is unrealistic. You'd be setting yourself a goal that no one can achieve. When you do have a suspicious thought – and eventually you're bound to – you'll feel disappointed, frustrated and ashamed.

Avoiding this feeling of failure is actually quite simple: choose goals you can expect to achieve. When you're deciding which goals to set yourself, start by thinking about the effect suspicious thoughts have on you. It's best to ground your goals in your experiences, rather than picking something fantastic but unrealistic or something that might be right for someone else but isn't really relevant to you. So if you find your suspicious thoughts getting in the way of your social life, you might want to have a goal to go out more. If you find your suspicious thoughts are all you think about, it would probably be good to have a goal to stop being so preoccupied by them.

Typical goals for dealing with suspicious thoughts

Here are some typical goals that people set themselves:

- I want my suspicious thoughts to occur less often.
- I want to be able to cope better with my suspicious thoughts.
- I'd like to reduce the distress they cause me.
- I want to stop believing that my fears might be true.
- I'd like to change the way I react.
- I want to get on with my life and stop these thoughts from interfering all the time.
- I want to stop avoiding social situations.
- I want to be able to relax with people rather than being suspicious of them.
- I need to understand why I have these thoughts, and then move on.
- I want to get into the habit of checking whether my fears are true rather than just assuming they are.
- I'd like to get more control over my suspiciousness.
- I want to enjoy my life more.

Write down your goals in your notebook or, if you prefer, in the space provided here:

Follow the ten steps we're going to present over the next chapters and you'll make real progress with your goals.

Step 1 Track your suspicious thoughts week by week

Keeping a record of your suspicious thoughts is the only sure way for you to see how much progress you're making. Most of us are generally not that great at recognising our achievements. When we think about how we're doing, it's all too easy to focus on what hasn't gone as well as we'd like, and to overlook all the good work we've done.

But if you regularly track your experience of suspicious thoughts, you'll have an accurate picture of how this has changed over time. People often forget how frequent and distressing their suspicious thoughts used to be. Your notebook will be a fantastic historical record, showing you just how far you've come – and how much further you want to go. It can also be useful in pinpointing what has helped most. You can see whether a particular exercise or change in behaviour has made a difference.

Exercise: Tracking your suspicious thoughts

We suggest you track your suspicious thoughts in the following way.

First, write down the suspicious thought that's worrying you most:

Now rate:

- How strongly you believe it (give a figure from 0 to 100 per cent) ________;
- How distressing you find it (give a figure from 0 to 10 with 0 meaning not distressing and 10 meaning extremely distressing) ________ ;
- The approximate number of times a day that you think about it ________.

Do this exercise at the end of each week. You can plot your progress by entering your ratings onto the following graphs:

Graph 1 How strongly you believe the thought.

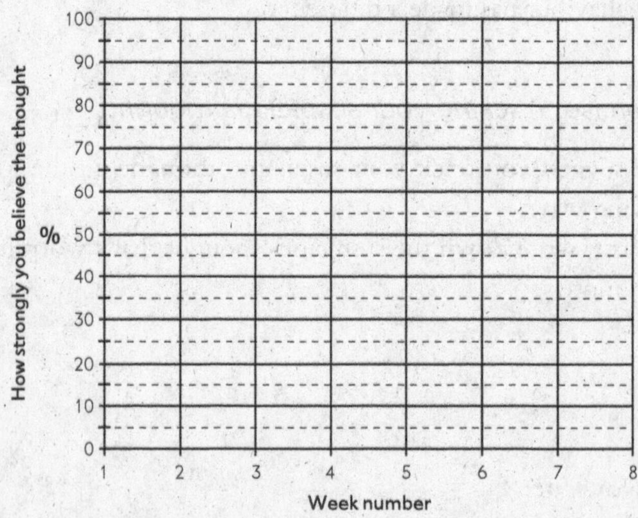

Graph 2 How distressing the thought is.

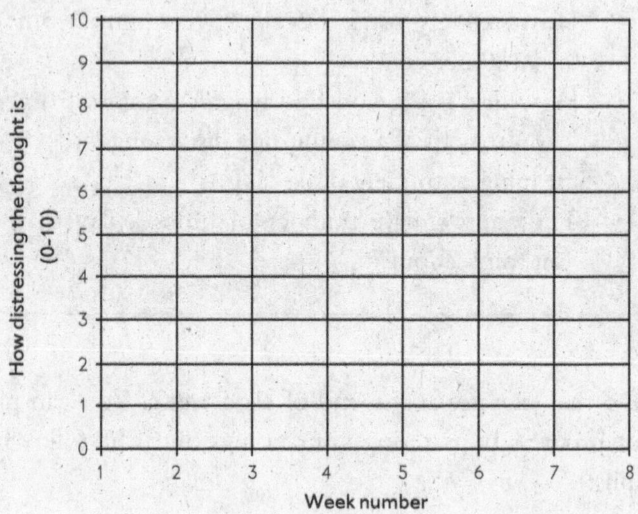

Graph 3 The approximate number of times a day you think about it.

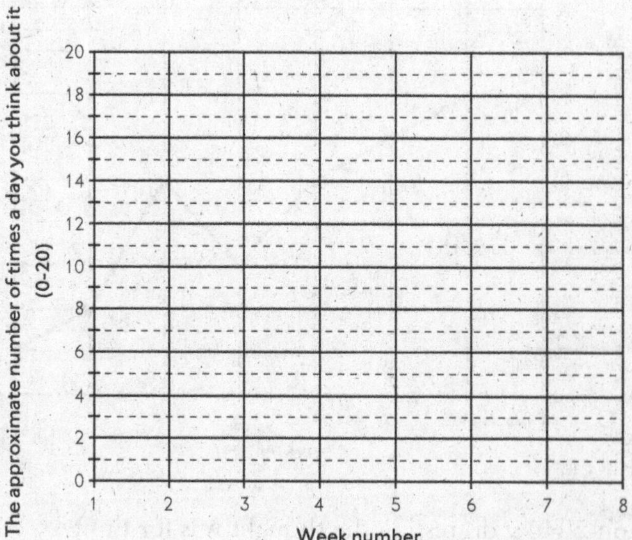

If you have another suspicious thought that's particularly concerning, you can also rate that and add the scores to the graphs.

The graphs below were drawn up by Emily as she monitored her suspicious thoughts over an eight-week period. She tracked the thought:

> *People laugh at me, or talk negatively about me, behind my back.*

You can see that Emily improved over time, though there was an occasional blip when she felt worse.

Graph 1 How strongly Emily believed the thought.

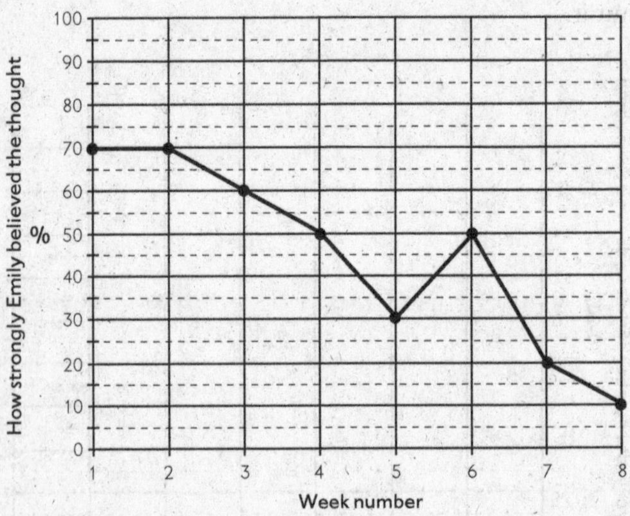

Graph 2 How distressing the thought was for Emily.

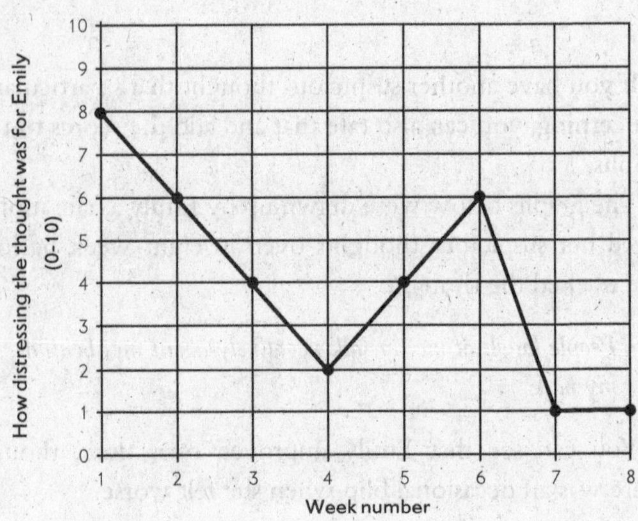

Graph 3 The approximate number of times a day Emily thought about it.

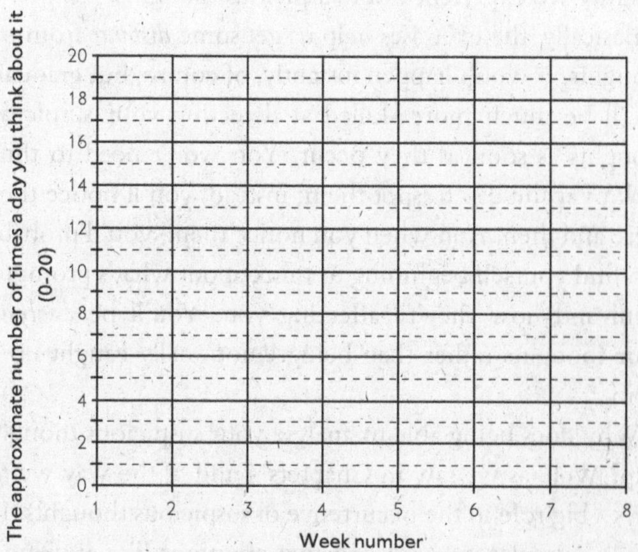

Step 2 Increase your understanding of your suspicious thoughts

Step 1 is all about tracking the effect that suspicious thoughts have on you. Step 2 is designed to help you *understand* these experiences.

To help you do this, we'd like you to try four exercises. If you stick with them, you'll increase your awareness of the factors that lead to your suspicious thoughts. You'll have a much clearer idea of why you have these experiences.

You'll also probably find that you're able to cope better with your suspicious thoughts. Many people tell us that they notice an improvement simply by doing these exercises. There's a reason for this: doing the exercises actually *changes* the way we experience our suspicious thoughts.

Basically, the exercises help us get some *distance* from our thoughts. It won't happen instantly, of course, but gradually you'll be much more skilled at detecting your suspicious thoughts as soon as they occur. You won't need to think back over the day to spot them; instead, you'll notice them there and then. And when you notice them, you'll probably also find yourself beginning to think about what's prompted them and how they're affecting you. You'll be *analysing* your thoughts rather than being emotionally caught up in them.

Why does being able to analyse your suspicious thoughts help? Well, as we saw in Chapters 4 and 5, the way we *feel* plays a big role in the occurrence of suspicious thoughts. It's often a circular process: negative emotions like anxiety or depression seem to prompt suspicious thoughts; the suspicious thoughts make us feel anxious or depressed, which then provokes more paranoia.

Taking a step back from our worries disrupts this vicious circle. Instead of getting distressed by our suspicious thoughts, we're concentrating on trying to understand them. And because we're less distressed, the suspicious thoughts have less to feed on. As a result, they're easier to manage and less likely to recur.

So there's a double incentive for you to do these exercises. They'll help you understand your suspicious thoughts – an essential step in your long-term effort to cope with your fears. But they'll also give you a more immediate boost, breaking the cycle of negative emotions that sustains and perpetuates your suspicious thoughts.

Exercise A: Keep a diary for a week

It's all too easy to forget the exact form our suspicious thoughts take, when they occur and how they affect us. But without these details, it's hard for us to really understand what's going on. So we suggest that you keep a diary. Start by doing so for a week. Make sure you fill it in every day when the experience is fresh in your mind. It's best to write up your diary at the same time each day – it'll help you make it part of your routine.

We've found the following format works well:

Date	Time	What was I doing?	How was I feeling?	What was my suspicious thought?	How did I react?

Here's an extract from Keith's diary:

Date	Time	What was I doing?	How was I feeling?	What was my suspicious thought?	How did I react?
Sunday 7th	3.00pm	At home, watching TV	Bored, a bit down	Found myself thinking about work. Worried about the treatment I was going to get from work mates tomorrow. My thought was: 'They all hate me. They're against me.'	Felt pretty stressed. Spent the next hour or so worrying.
Sunday 7th	Evening	Ironing clothes for week	Still stressed at prospect of work	Thought about the report that my boss has asked me to write. Meeting with him on Wednesday. Am pleased with it but had the thought: 'No matter what I write he's going to pick it to pieces. He has it in for me'. I even thought then: 'He might set the others on to me to	Got angry with my boss! Then was angry with myself for caring.

Monday 8th	5.30am	In bed, just woken up	Very tense	Had a sense that today was going to be hard. Remembered how well I used to get on with everyone and spent a long time thinking about how I got from there to here. Thought: 'This hassle is going to keep on going on. It's psychological warfare.' Carried on worrying all the way to work.	Sad. Anxious about the day ahead.
Monday 8th	9.00pm	At home, reading the paper	Quite relaxed, but very tired	Struck me that today had actually been fine at work. Had gone out for drink with team at lunchtime (Chris's birthday). All very friendly. But boss wasn't there and I thought: 'If my boss was here then he'd say something to get at me.'	Cross at boss, cross with myself for having these thoughts even after a good day.

After you've kept your diary for a week, read it through a couple of times and think about these questions:

What triggers my suspicious thoughts?

- *Are my suspicious thoughts more likely to occur in particular situations?*
- *Am I more likely to have these thoughts when I'm busy or when I'm not doing much?*
- *What kind of a mood am I in just before I have a suspicious thought? Is it different from normal?*
- *Do I feel different inside just before I have a suspicious thought?*
- *Do I tend to be expecting trouble or hostility from other people before I have a suspicious thought?*
- *Are any negative or unhappy images going through my mind in the run-up to a suspicious thought?*

How do I react to my suspicious thoughts?

- *Do I feel anxious when I have a suspicious thought?*
- *Do I feel more anxious than normal?*
- *Do I start to panic when I have these thoughts?*
- *Do I try to get away from the situation I'm in?*

- *Do I treat the thought as if it's true?*
- *Do I try to think through what's happening?*
- *What do I do to try to cope with the thought?*

Exercise B: Write about your suspicious thoughts

We'd like you to have a go at writing a description of your experiences with suspicious thoughts. Concentrate on what was happening on one recent occasion and how you felt. Don't try to analyse things. What we want you to put down on paper are the exact details of your experience – and it's hard to do that if you're also trying to work out what it all means. Just describing your experiences in this very focused way will help you learn about your fears and the kinds of judgements and assumptions you make while having suspicious thoughts.

One technique that people sometimes find helpful is to imagine that they're writing a movie script. You need to tell the director (or maybe the actor playing you) exactly what's going on, and exactly what you're thinking, at every moment – and in chronological order. Describe the scene in as much detail as you can. Try to capture every twist and turn of your thoughts and feelings. Write down your thoughts, even if they now seem embarrassing. If any images went through your mind, try to describe those as clearly as you can. Remember, what you're trying to get down is *the way it felt from moment to moment* – don't worry about anything else at this point.

Pick a recent occasion when you've had a troubling suspicious thought. When you've finished describing your experience (don't write more than a side of paper), try to do it again for two more episodes. As an example, here's something written by Emily:

A drinks party for Carrie. She was leaving the firm – relocating to New Zealand. About thirty of us in the pub. Friday night so the place was packed even without us lot. Very hot. Everyone in weekend mode. High spirits. Had a very nice time chatting to people.

After a while found myself with Carrie, who I like, and Francis (one of the senior partners). Francis is okay but I've always found him a bit intimidating. Anyhow, Carrie, Francis, and I were standing there talking and he said he was really sorry to see Carrie go. Working with her had always been a pleasure. He was sure she was going to be a huge success in New Zealand. I found myself trying to remember a single word of praise that Francis had ever given me. We've worked together quite a bit but I couldn't think of anything. I suddenly felt angry and upset. I felt that Francis clearly didn't rate me, just like the other senior partners. Told myself that he was just saying the sort of thing everyone said at a leaving do – in fact, I'd already heard lots of comments like this that evening and none of them had bothered me.

I knew I was reacting unreasonably, but that didn't help. I had another of the thoughts I quite often have: everyone thinks I'm rubbish, they want me to leave. Then Francis (who'd been looking straight at Carrie) glanced at me and I was convinced that this was his way of pointing out to me that his little compliments to Carrie were meant to send a message to me. That did it: I knew I had to get out of there before I burst into tears or said something stupid. I went to the loo and hoped that Francis hadn't been able to tell how much he'd got to me.

As usual in these situations, I felt ridiculous and ashamed of myself – and really disappointed that an enjoyable evening had ended badly again.

Exercise C: Go looking for a suspicious thought

This exercise is one to try when you're feeling confident.

The exercises we've described so far are all retrospective: they involve looking back at suspicious thoughts after they've occurred. But this one is a bit different – and at first it might sound a little strange! We'd like you to try to have a suspicious thought. Think of a situation that's likely to provoke your fears – and then put yourself into that situation.

Why on earth would I want to do that, you might well be thinking! Well, it's a fantastic learning opportunity. It's not something to try if you're feeling down or anxious or struggling to cope (if you are, skip to Exercise D). But when things are going better, it gives you the perfect chance to observe yourself as you experience a suspicious thought. Because you know the thought is likely to be coming, you can be ready for it. Instead of trying hours later to remember what happened, you get a *real time* insight into the triggers, the feelings and your reactions. It's your own personal show, a chance to settle into your seat and watch what it's like to have a paranoid thought. When you're doing this, try to be aware of how you feel before going into the situation, the internal and external experiences that are leading you to think suspiciously, and your reaction (your thoughts, feelings and behaviour). The information you get from this will help you in the next exercise, which is all about looking at the causes of your suspicious thoughts.

Exercise D: The causes of a suspicious thought

As we've seen, suspicious thoughts don't just arrive out of the blue. Instead, they are the product of a combination of powerful factors. If we can understand how these factors combine, we'll find it easier to deal with our suspicious thoughts.

In Chapters 4 and 5, we set out the typical causes of paranoid thoughts. Now we want you to take that theoretical knowledge and use it to understand your own experiences. Look back at the suspicious thoughts you drew on for Exercises A, B and C. Choose the one that affected you most strongly and have a go at filling in the blank diagrams opposite. Try to fill in the diagram without looking back at the previous chapters. Once you've had a go at this, look back at Chapters 4 and 5 to see whether you've forgotten an important factor.

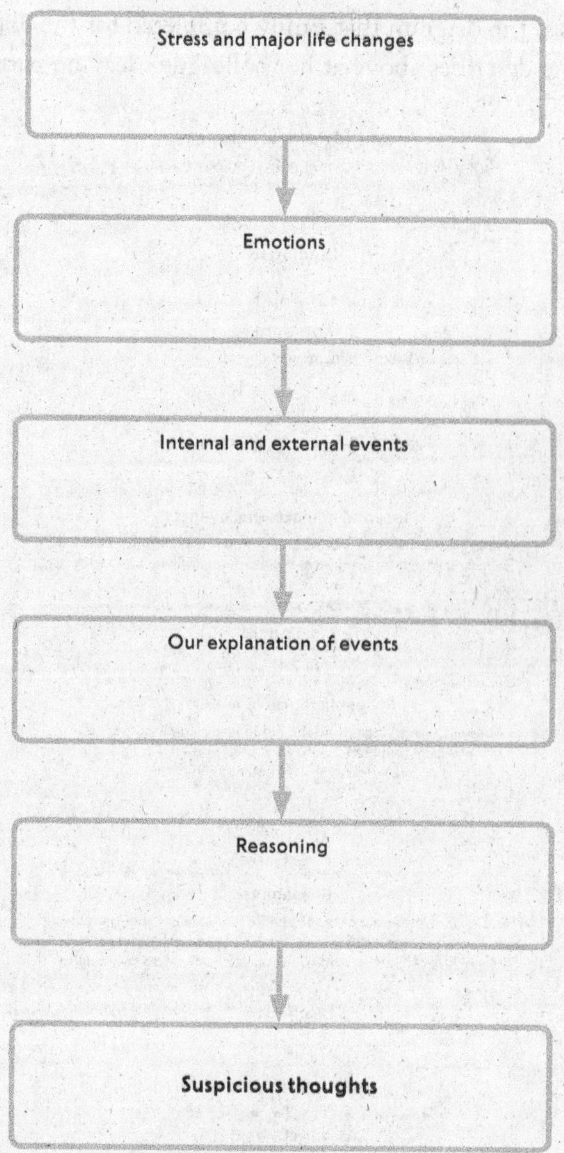
Stress and major life changes
Emotions
Internal and external events
Our explanation of events
Reasoning
Suspicious thoughts

This is the diagram that Emily completed for the experience she describes above at her colleague's leaving party:

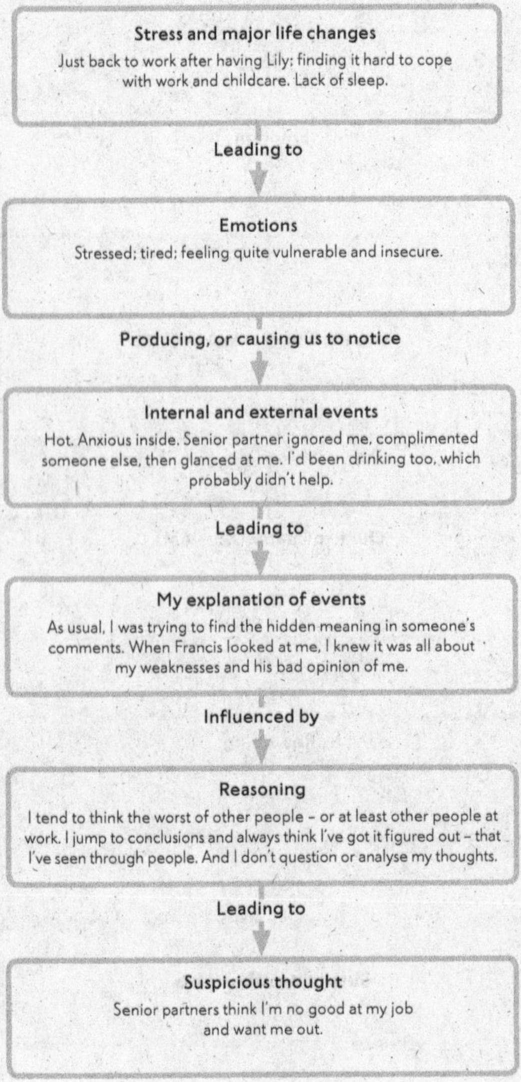

Stress and major life changes
Just back to work after having Lily: finding it hard to cope with work and childcare. Lack of sleep.

Leading to

Emotions
Stressed; tired; feeling quite vulnerable and insecure.

Producing, or causing us to notice

Internal and external events
Hot. Anxious inside. Senior partner ignored me, complimented someone else, then glanced at me. I'd been drinking too, which probably didn't help.

Leading to

My explanation of events
As usual, I was trying to find the hidden meaning in someone's comments. When Francis looked at me, I knew it was all about my weaknesses and his bad opinion of me.

Influenced by

Reasoning
I tend to think the worst of other people – or at least other people at work. I jump to conclusions and always think I've got it figured out – that I've seen through people. And I don't question or analyse my thoughts.

Leading to

Suspicious thought
Senior partners think I'm no good at my job and want me out.

Once you've completed the two steps we've described in this chapter you'll have:

- An up-to-date record of how much you're affected by suspicious thoughts and the way your experience changes over time;
- A greater understanding of how your suspicious thoughts are caused and how you react to them;
- Gained some distance from your paranoid thoughts by learning how to observe and analyse them.

In the next chapters, we'll set out the remaining eight steps that will help you overcome your suspicious thoughts.

Chapter summary

- There are ten practical steps you can take to overcome your suspicious thoughts.
- The first two steps are designed to help you develop a detailed understanding of how and when your suspicious thoughts affect you.
- To gain this understanding, you need to become a detached observer of your anxieties.
- We have a much better chance of succeeding with these steps if we can support them with the right kind of attitude and behaviours.

7

Reducing worry

Introduction

If we're prone to suspicious thoughts, it's very likely that we'll also worry a lot. Again and again, our thoughts will focus on our fears. All the research suggests that these two ways of thinking – paranoia and worry – tend to go together.

We all know what it feels like to worry, but how do psychologists define this most common of human experiences? Well, worry is a kind of repetitive negative thinking. We peer into the future and ask ourselves: *what will go wrong and what will follow when it does?* We *catastrophise*. Disaster, no matter how unlikely in reality, seems to lie in wait around every corner. And worry, of course, *feels* awful – a horrible, nagging form of distress that can dominate every waking moment.

The more we worry, the more likely it is that we'll experience suspicious thoughts, and the greater the chance that these thoughts will persist. This is what scientists call a **dose-response** relationship: increase the amount of X and you'll produce more of Y.

But the good news is that the reverse holds true. By reducing our level of worry – and that is definitely feasible – we can loosen the grip of our suspicious thoughts. Curtail worry and we also help defuse our paranoia. So Step 3 of our ten-step programme will show how we can reduce the amount of time we spend thinking about our fears.

Worry and suspicious thoughts: personal accounts

'. . . sit and think. Then get paranoider and paranoider and paranoider and paranoider.'

'It's totally um . . . drowning. The fears.'

'It's a general feeling that your state of mind is . . . er . . . in control of you rather than you in control of it, you know.'

'I can't get away from it, here there or anywhere, it's always around.'

'When other situations are presented to me because I'm worrying about that as well, I can't handle both and it goes into overdrive.'

Learning about worry

Before we focus on the techniques you can use to overcome your worrying, we'll spend a little time exploring what worry is and how it can affect us.

When we worry we think about the consequences of something bad happening:

What if my boss thinks my work isn't up to scratch?
What if I've done something to offend my friends?
What if I miss my train?

Let's play the *What if* game with a trivial negative event – in this case, accidentally spilling some food on our clothes at lunch.

- What bad thing might happen if you spill your food? Write it down.
- Then what bad thing might happen? Write it down.
- Then what bad thing might happen? Write it down.
- Then what bad thing might happen? Write it down.
- Then what bad thing might happen? Write it down.

Here's what we came up with when we did this exercise:

- What bad thing might happen if you spill your food? *It makes a mark on my shirt.*

- Then what bad thing might happen? *I'd look messy and unprofessional.*
- Then what bad thing might happen? *My boss might notice.*
- Then what bad thing might happen? *She'd think badly of me.*
- Then what bad thing might happen? *It might influence the way she feels about me – and my contract is due for renewal soon.*
- Then what bad thing might happen? *I might not get my contract renewed. I'd be out of work.*

So being a bit clumsy at lunchtime has cost us our job! This is pretty far-fetched, of course, but actually that's the way worry works. We spend a lot of time fretting about things that are highly unlikely to happen. We don't take a balanced view of the situation; instead *we focus on the negative*. How often do we spend ages worrying about something and then decide that everything is bound to work out okay? Not very often! And the more we worry, the worse we expect things to turn out: *worry feeds on worry*. Of course spilling some food is a fairly trivial event. If we can worry a minor mishap like that into unemployment imagine where our fears might take us with a bigger problem . . .

Why do we worry?

Given that worrying can be such an unpleasant experience, why do so many of us spend so much time doing it?

The answer is simple: we worry because we believe that it will help somehow. That may surprise you; after all, worry generally seems like an automatic process. We don't tend to sit down and think: *Right, what shall I worry about now?* It just seems to happen. However, positive beliefs about worry are often buried pretty far down. We may not be aware of them until we start to reflect on our experience. But these deeply rooted ideas can allow worry to become a habit.

Do you hold any of these positive beliefs about worry?

Positive belief	Tick if you believe
Worry keeps me safe	
Worry prevents bad things from happening	
Worry helps me to avoid problems in the future	
Worry keeps me organised	
Worry prepares me for the worst	
Worry motivates me	
Worry helps me to cope	
If I did not worry I'd make more mistakes	
Worry is my way of taking responsibility	
Any others?	

These kinds of belief make us vulnerable to a vicious cycle of worry. Feeling threatened triggers our positive ideas about worry. But of course worry doesn't make us feel safe; it *magnifies* our sense of danger. And consequently we worry even more:

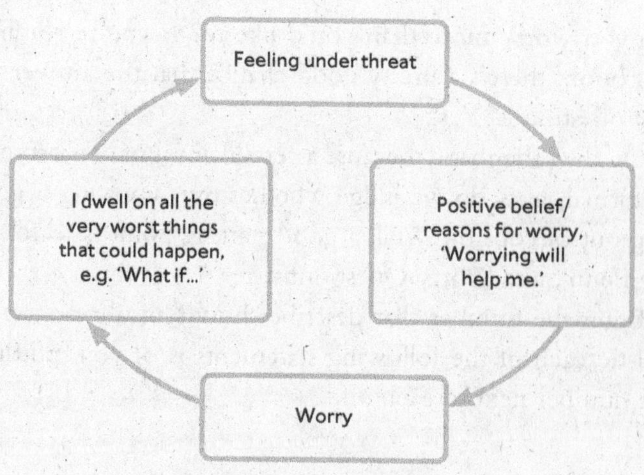

How can we break out of this cycle?

The key is to understand that our positive beliefs about worry can't be relied upon. Far from making us feel safer, worry increases our sense of danger. The view of the world it gives us is skewed: negative events seem much more likely than they really are. If you doubt it, try watching the movie *Jaws* and then contemplating a dip in the ocean! The chances of being attacked by a shark are tiny, but it's very difficult to keep that in mind if you've recently watched

Spielberg's movie. All of which means that in order to develop a more helpful attitude to our fears, we need to take control of our worrying.

How much do you worry?

Do you worry more than you'd like to? If you're reading this book, there's a pretty good chance that the answer to that question is 'Yes'.

On the other hand, because a certain amount of worrying is normal, how do we judge whether our worrying is getting out of control? Well, a good starting point is to fill in the Penn State Worry Questionnaire.

Enter the number that describes how typical or characteristic each of the following statements is of you, putting the number next to each one.

1	2	3	4	5
Not at all typical		Somewhat typical		Very typical

1. If I don't have enough time to do everything, I don't worry about it. ____
2. My worries overwhelm me. ____
3. I don't tend to worry about things. ____
4. Many situations make me worry. ____
5. I know I shouldn't worry about things, but I just can't help it. ____
6. When I'm under pressure, I worry a lot. ____

7. I am always worrying about something. ____
8. I find it easy to dismiss worrisome thoughts. ____
9. As soon as I finish one task, I start to worry about something else. ____
10. I never worry about anything. ____
11. When there is nothing more I can do about a concern, I don't worry about it any more. ____
12. I've been a worrier all my life. ____
13. I notice that I have been worrying about things. ____
14. Once I start worrying, I can't stop. ____
15. I worry all the time. ____
16. I worry about projects until they are all done. ____

Penn State Worry Questionnaire: Meyer, T. J., Miller, M. L., Metzger, R. L., & Borkovec, T. D. (1990). Development and validation of the Penn State Worry Questionnaire. Behaviour Research & Therapy, 28, 487–95.

Now add up your scores for each statement. Questions 3, 8, 10 and 11 are *reverse scored*: if for example you put 5, for scoring purposes the item is counted as 1. Scores can range from 18 to 80.

People with worry problems usually score above 46. But if your total is on the high side, remember that this doesn't necessarily mean that you have a problem. To be absolutely sure, it's best to discuss your situation with a qualified professional.

Step 3 Spending less time preoccupied by our fears

Using worry periods

Almost everyone worries from time to time. So it's probably unrealistic to aim for a completely worry-free existence. The trick is to reduce the amount of time you spend worrying. You can train yourself to do this, and this is where **worry periods** come in.

Worry periods are short spaces of time in which you give yourself permission to worry. Don't try to fight your anxieties; let them have full rein. But the rules are that you have to stop when time is up – and you mustn't worry at other times.

There are a couple of planning steps you need to take to maximise the potential of worry periods.

- First, *decide on a time and place.* To start with, aim to devote fifteen to twenty minutes to worry every day. To help you get into the habit, choose the same time each day. Whatever works for you is fine, though it's best not to pick a slot too close to bedtime – if it's the last thing you think about at night, you might find it hard to get to sleep. (Some people prefer a longer session, or opt for two sessions per day. Feel free to follow your instincts.)

Where should you worry? It's a good idea to choose somewhere that's slightly uncomfortable – maybe a hard chair, or a step on the stairs, or the floor. Steer clear of relaxing places such as your bed or a sofa. You don't want to give yourself any incentive to keep worrying once your allotted time is up, and you don't want to associate worry with spaces in which you normally unwind.

- Second, *decide what you're going to do if you catch yourself worrying at other times.* When are you most vulnerable to worry, and what could you do to lessen the risk? Often worry creeps in when our attention isn't especially engaged by what we're doing: we might be watching TV, for example, or leafing through the newspaper. So aim to schedule as many absorbing activities into your day as possible. Physical exercise is a particularly effective deterrent for worry – and it'll also help you sleep better.

If you do find yourself worrying outside your worry periods, simply write down what's bugging you and tell yourself you'll return to it at the appropriate time. If you're finding it tough to postpone your worry like this, ask yourself why. For example, are your positive beliefs about worry still strong? Don't let worry dominate you: question it!

Here's what Keith told us about the effect suspicious thoughts had on him:

> *You asked me how much time I used to spend worrying. Well, basically it took up all of my spare time. At least that's the way it felt when I was at my lowest. If I wasn't totally preoccupied with whatever I was doing, I'd find my worries creeping in again. Then it was more or less impossible to think about anything else. It felt a bit like an addiction. I couldn't give it up, even though I was desperate.*

When we're worried about something, getting that anxiety out of our minds for even a short time can seem the hardest thing in the world. As Keith says, worry can be so powerful and uncontrollable that it feels like an addiction.

But just like an addiction, worry can be beaten. We asked Keith to save up his worrying for a daily thirty-minute 'worry period'. So if he found himself worrying at any other time, he had to try to postpone his worry till later. Keith's task was to notice when he started to worry but, instead of thinking about it, he had to write it down and save it for his worry period. We suggested that he did his worrying at the same time every day and Keith chose 6.30–7 p.m., just after he'd got home from work.

> *It took a bit of time to get the hang of it, but after a few days I got pretty good at postponing my worrying. I said to myself, 'Not now. I'll deal with you later.' At the beginning I'd write down the worry in my notebook so I*

> *didn't forget it. I don't do that now. When I got back from work, I'd sit on a kitchen chair, and set my alarm clock for thirty minutes' time. I actually used to look forward to my worrying time – it sounds strange, but it was nice feeling that it was okay to worry for that half hour. I didn't feel guilty or embarrassed like I usually did when I worried. In the early weeks I had no problem filling the half hour. It could be a struggle to stop worrying when the alarm went. After a while though I either ran out of energy with time left or didn't start at all. I told myself I'd do the worry period tomorrow, but when tomorrow came I sometimes didn't do it then either. Maybe I was weaning myself off worrying.*

Try using worry periods yourself. You may well find that, like Keith, you stop needing them. Worrying can come to seem much less important. And even if that doesn't happen for you, worry periods will help you get on with your life without the constant nagging distraction of your anxieties.

Replacing worry periods with problem-solving

When we worry, we give ourselves a skewed perspective on the world. We focus on the bad stuff – all the terrible things that might happen to us if things go wrong.

It can be really helpful to correct that one-eyed view. Instead of spending all our worry period dwelling on the negative, we need to open up to the constructive things we can do to make our lives better. In particular, let's start to see our suspicious thoughts – and the worries they trigger – as *problems we can solve.* When you feel ready, aim to replace these worry periods with **problem-solving periods.**

For instance, you could think about the events that normally spark your paranoia. It may be when you think people are getting at you or being too intrusive, or when you're feeling really tired or stressed. What we need you to do is change the way you respond to these triggers. Instead of worrying about them, think about how you could deal with these experiences differently.

Problem-solving is all about taking a logical approach to dealing with issues. And because it's logical, there's no mystery: we can learn how to do it. Follow the steps we set out below (make sure you write down your answers):

1. **Define the problem** as specifically as you can.
2. **Think of as many solutions** to the problem as you possibly can. Try to remember what's worked for you in the past. If you think it might be useful, ask someone you trust for advice. What would you tell someone who came to you with the same problem?
3. **Weigh up the pros and cons** of each of the possible solutions.
4. **Choose the solution** you think is best and decide how you're going to carry it out. Try to anticipate the problems you might face with it, and think through how you might deal with them.
5. **Try out the solution** you've chosen. Afterwards, have a think about how well it's worked. If things haven't gone as well as you'd have liked, start the problem-solving process again.

Here's what happened when Keith tried problem-solving:

1. *The problem is that when my boss makes a remark about me or my work in front of other people I assume he's getting at me.*

2. *I can think of four possible solutions:*

    - *Challenge him in the meeting.*
    - *Have a word with him in private and explain the way his behaviour makes me feel.*
    - *Ask the other folk at work whether they think he's getting at me.*
    - *Try not to react in my normal way. I'd like to be able to tell myself it's nothing and that I'm just imagining things as usual. I'd like these sorts of incident to seem really trivial to me. Actually, I'd like to reach the stage where I'm not bothered even if he really is having a go at me.*

3. *Challenging him in the meeting shows I'm not scared of him. It puts me in the driving seat for once. It'll show everyone that I can look after myself. On the other hand, I might make a complete idiot of myself in front of the whole team. I'll probably be so nervous I won't be able to say what I want to say to him. And what if I'm wrong about what he's doing? That's going to be even more embarrassing.*

    Having a word with him in private feels like a much more sensible idea. We can have an honest, man-to-man conversation. Clear the air and all that. But I'm worried about saying too much or saying the wrong thing. I don't trust myself to stay calm in that situation. And I don't think he'll be very interested in the way I feel. He's not exactly the touchy-feely type.

If I speak to the guys at work, I'll get a different perspective on all this. I feel like I'm far too close to it to really know for sure what's happening. If they tell me they don't think he's putting me down, I'll know that I'm just overreacting. If they reckon he is, then I'll know I'm not imagining it all. I'll know I'm not crazy. The only drawback I can see is that they might think I really am mad! And I don't honestly know whether I've got the nerve to talk to other people about this stuff: it feels too personal.

If I try to deal with it on my own, I don't get other people's perspective. It just stays as my problem, which is a bit lonely. But at least I don't have to worry about other people's reactions. I don't have to summon up the courage to talk to anyone else. I'll be sorting it out for myself, which will feel good. Plus this is something I've been trying out lately and things have gone quite well.

4 *I've decided to go with option four. The next time my boss does something to wind me up, I'll try to just let it go. I might make a note of a couple of phrases I can use – just in case I get upset or flustered and forget what I'm trying to do. If I do write something down, I don't want the person sitting next to me to see it.*

5 *At our next team meeting, I felt there were a couple of moments when my boss might have been having a dig at me. And later in the same meeting I thought he was maybe ignoring me. I tried really hard not to let these things get to me. I wrote in my notebook, 'it doesn't matter'. And I looked at that, and repeated it in my head, over and over. And then I tried to concentrate on remembering all the things Carrie (that's my daughter) and I had done together the other weekend. I might have been in that meeting room physically, but I did my best to be somewhere else in my mind. It worked pretty well – better than I'd expected. I suppose it might have looked as if I was daydreaming, but I won't have been the only one!*

Many people find this problem-solving approach helps reduce the number of suspicious thoughts they have. And that usually means reducing their anxiety and worry too. And if that isn't a recommendation to give problem-solving a try, we don't know what is!

Accepting uncertainty

Most of us are wary of uncertainty. We want stability. We want predictability. We want to be assured that the way our world looks when we get up in the morning is the way it will look when we go to bed. And if change occurs, we prefer it to be on our terms.

Life, however, tends to have other ideas! Things don't always go to plan. The unexpected happens, whether we like it or not. And because we know this, we may find ourselves worrying about the future. Indeed, research has shown that people who worry a lot tend to be particularly uncomfortable about uncertainty.

Have a think about your own worries: does uncertainty play a part? Does your anxiety stem in part from the feeling that you don't know how things will turn out? And does that feeling result in you fearing the worst? Does not knowing frighten you, or make you stressed?

We have to come to terms with uncertainty. We have to accept that no action is 100 per cent risk-free, and that we can't totally control events, no matter how much we try. Besides, would constant certainty be such a great thing? Wouldn't life become stale and boring? Wouldn't we end up yearning for the unexpected?

Our life, just like everyone else's, will include highs and lows. No matter how much we worry, we can't know what's in store for us. And we can't prevent problems happening just by worrying about them. So instead of dwelling on possible – though unlikely – disasters in an uncertain future, it's far better to focus on the present. And especially to concentrate on and celebrate the positive things in our lives right now.

Chapter summary

- Worry and paranoia tend to go together. By reducing our level of worry we can also overcome our suspicious thoughts.
- We worry because we believe it will help us. We need to challenge our positive beliefs about worry.
- Worry periods are a great way of controlling our worrying.
- In time we can aim to replace our worry periods with problem-solving sessions.
- Accepting uncertainty can be an important part of our strategy to overcome worry.

8

Sleeping better

Are you getting enough sleep? If not you are most definitely not alone: around one in three people have significant problems sleeping.

All of us, though, know how awful it can feel when we don't get at least close to the magical eight hours. Life suddenly seems an uphill struggle. The simplest tasks become too much for us. Tiredness stokes negative thoughts and feelings: irritability, anxiety, unhappiness. We can find it hard to concentrate or make decisions. Odd sensations – like the anomalous experiences we mentioned in Chapter 2 – can occur. And nothing can make things better except our bed!

Why does lack of sleep tend to affect us in this unpleasant way? The answer is that we are creatures of habit. The human sleep cycle is hundreds of thousands of years old and therefore, as you might imagine, deeply engrained. For the past 4.5 billion years the Earth has spun on its axis, alternating night and day roughly every twenty-four hours. This daily cycle is hard-wired into our bodies, with changes in the environment – especially the level of daylight – determining our sleep, eating and even body temperature. These are our **circadian rhythms** ('circadian' comes from the Latin words meaning 'about a day').

Circadian rhythms are not an exclusively human phenomenon. They're just as important for other animals and plants too, and for pretty much all forms of life on the planet. And because they're so key to our functioning, our system doesn't like it when the pattern is disrupted – for example, when we don't get sufficient good-quality sleep at night.

What has all this got to do with suspicious thoughts? Well, the negative thoughts and feelings sleeplessness often produces are known to make paranoia worse. Our research suggests that insomnia (the clinical term for difficulty getting to sleep, or staying asleep) can be a significant factor in the development of paranoid thoughts. There are plenty of compelling reasons, then, for tackling any sleep problems you may have. Later in this chapter we'll explain exactly how you can do so, but first let's take a look at the nature of sleep.

The basics of sleep

Every creature on the planet needs to sleep, though the specifics vary quite a lot: for example, bats sleep for an enviable twenty hours in every day while giraffes make do with around two hours a night. How much sleep should you be getting each night? Everyone will have their own preference, but age plays a big part. Generally speaking the older we become the less sleep we require, as you can see from the table below:

Age	**Average amount of sleep needed per day**
Birth–2 months	10.5–18 hours
2–12 months	14–15 hours
12–18 months	13–15 hours
18 months–3 years	12–14 hours
3–5 years	11–13 hours
5–12 years	9–11 hours
Teenagers	8–10 hours
Adults (18–65)	7–9 hours
Older adults (65 and above)	6–7 hours

These figures don't tell the whole story about sleep, though. This is because there are actually five stages of sleep and we cycle through them several times each night. It takes about ninety minutes to move through the full cycle: from stages one and two when we're dropping off, to stages three and four when we're deeply asleep, to the REM sleep of stage five, when our brain activity is at the same kind of level as when we're awake. Getting to the end of each cycle is a vulnerable time for our sleep: it's quite possible that we'll wake up. And that chance increases with each completed cycle.

People vary in the amount of sleep they need, but they

also differ in *when* they prefer to sleep (scientists call this our 'chronotype'). You might be a lark, functioning best if you're early to bed and early to rise. Perhaps you're an owl – at your sharpest at night. Or maybe, like many people, you're situated somewhere in between these two extremes.

Our sleep is regulated by two key brain processes. The first is something called the **sleep homeostat** and it's pretty simple in principle: the longer we've been awake, the sleepier we'll feel.

The second process is our **internal clock** (the circadian rhythm we mentioned earlier in this chapter). It's tied very much to the presence of daylight, meaning that we are naturally programmed to sleep at night. The darker it is, the more the brain releases a hormone called melatonin, and the drowsier we feel as a consequence.

To sleep really well we need to get these two processes into harmony. We want our sleep homeostat to tell us to head to bed at night-time and not, for example, at lunch time. Our drive for sleep should kick in when it's dark. That's what our internal clock is expecting!

How well are you sleeping?

If you think you may be suffering from insomnia have a go at this assessment. It won't take you long. For each of the seven questions circle the number that best describes your experiences *over the past two weeks.*

Questions 1–3 ask for information about the current severity of your insomnia problem(s).

<table>
<tr><th>Insomnia problem</th><th>None</th><th>Mild</th><th>Moderate</th><th>Severe</th><th>Very Severe</th></tr>
<tr><td>1 Difficulty falling asleep?</td><td>0</td><td>1</td><td>2</td><td>3</td><td>4</td></tr>
<tr><td>2 Difficulty staying asleep?</td><td>0</td><td>1</td><td>2</td><td>3</td><td>4</td></tr>
<tr><td>3 Problems waking up too early?</td><td>0</td><td>1</td><td>2</td><td>3</td><td>4</td></tr>
<tr><td colspan="6">4 How satisfied/dissatisfied are you with your current sleep pattern?
Very satisfied 0 Satisfied 1 Moderately satisfied 2 Dissatisfied 3 Very dissatisfied 4</td></tr>
<tr><td colspan="6">5 How noticeable to others do you think your sleep problem is in terms of impairing the quality of your life?
Not at all 0 A little 1 Somewhat 2 Much 3 Very much 4</td></tr>
<tr><td colspan="6">6 How worried/distressed are you about your current sleep problem?
Not at all 0 A little 1 Somewhat 2 Much 3 Very much 4</td></tr>
<tr><td colspan="6">7 To what extent do you consider your sleep problem to interfere with your daily functioning (e.g. daytime fatigue, mood, ability to function at work/daily chores, concentration, memory, mood, etc.) currently?
Not at all 0 A little 1 Somewhat 2 Much 3 Very much 4</td></tr>
</table>

Insomnia Severity Index (Bastien *et al*, 2001)

When you've answered all seven questions, add up your score. A total of 15 or more suggests that the problem is significant enough to warrant a diagnosis of insomnia, with 22 or more indicating a severe case.

Step 4 Improving your sleep

If you're happy with your sleeping feel free to skip the rest of this chapter and head for Step 5. But if things aren't going as well as you'd like the next pages offer a tried-and-tested strategy to improve your sleep.

First, let's look at the basics: five quick wins for better sleep:

Get the light right

As we've seen, our body clock uses light levels to orient itself. We're programmed to sleep when it's dark (i.e. night) and be alert and active when the sun comes up. Of course, this process was a lot more straightforward before humans devised so many sources of artificial light. Watching television or looking at a computer screen close to bedtime, for example, sends our body the wrong signals: the light tells us that we need to be awake. So keep the light levels low as you wind down for the night. And aim to kick-start your system in the morning by getting out into the daylight. Even on a cloudy day, light intensity outside is around five times higher than what we get indoors with the electric lights on.

Exercise!

There are lots of good reasons to be physically active, but better sleep is perhaps one of the less well known. Think of your own experience: have you noticed that you sleep more soundly when you've been exercising? Try to build in around thirty minutes of physical activity every day. Remember that it doesn't have to be sport: a brisk walk or session of gardening or housework will do the job equally well. What you're after is aerobic exercise: raising your heart rate for a sustained period. But don't exercise close to bedtime; you'll be firing up your system just at the time when you want it to be slowing down.

Eat regular meals

You may wonder what eating has to do with sleeping. But we're unlikely to enjoy a good night's rest if we've eaten a lot late in the evening – or if, on the other hand, we've not eaten enough throughout the day. So it's best to aim for nutritious meals, evenly spaced throughout the day. And we shouldn't underestimate the importance of eating for our body clock. Regular meals help establish and reinforce our daily rhythm. Breakfast in particular is key, so make it a central part of your morning routine – up at the same time each day, followed by a wash or shower, a healthy, low-fat breakfast, and a walk. You'll soon notice the benefits!

Cut out caffeine, nicotine and alcohol in the evening

Caffeine and nicotine are both *stimulants*: they produce a state of enhanced alertness in our mind and body. As you might expect, this isn't ideal preparation for sleep! If you're having problems sleeping, we recommend that you avoid caffeine and nicotine in the evening. Remember that caffeine isn't only found in coffee: tea and most cola drinks, for example, also contain plenty of it.

Alcohol affects the body in a very different way: it's a *depressant* rather than a stimulant. What this means is that it dampens down our nervous system, slowing our physical and psychological reactions. This might seem like the perfect recipe for sleep, and it's true that drinking can certainly help us to nod off. But alcohol interferes with the sleep cycle we described earlier in this chapter. So while we might crash out after a few drinks, we won't get the kind of deep sleep that we need in order to feel rested the following day.

Develop a wind-down routine

New parents are often advised that a nightly wind-down routine, perhaps involving a bath, a milky drink and a storybook, will help their children fall asleep faster. It's much the same for adults. The details may vary, but you should choose activities that you find calming. Make them a habit: by repeating them each night your mind and body will learn that these are the signals for sleep.

Once you've put these five strategies in place it's time to move on to the next technique. This is all about *teaching yourself to associate bed with sleep*.

That may seem odd. *Of course I associate my bed with sleep!*, you may be thinking. But if we're struggling to cope with insomnia, sleep can be the last thing we think of in connection with bed. Anxiety, worry, frustration, exhaustion, unhappiness? Absolutely. Restful sleep? Sadly not.

How do we change things? How do we restore the psychological connection between our bed and peaceful, restorative sleep? There are four steps:

1. Decide on appropriate times for going to bed and getting up in the morning – and stick to them.
2. If you've not fallen asleep within fifteen to twenty minutes, get out of bed.
3. Only use your bed for sleep.
4. Don't nap in the daytime.

Let's look at each of these in more detail.

Decide on appropriate times for going to bed and getting up in the morning – and stick to them. This is all about getting used to sleeping at a time that suits our natural body clock. So fix an appropriate time for going to bed, probably somewhere between 10.30 p.m. and midnight. Choose a time when you're usually feeling sleepy. Lead up to it with your wind-down routine. Then decide on a getting up time around seven or eight hours later, building in your wake-up routine (shower, breakfast, walk).

Don't be tempted by your alarm's snooze button – falling back to sleep when you've just woken up will send your physiological system haywire.

Once you've selected your times it's really important to stick to them. That means resisting the urge to lie in – which can be tough, for sure. But keep in mind that it's only a temporary measure. What you're doing here is developing positive habits. Once you've done the hard work you'll be able to reap the rewards for a long time to come.

What if at the moment you're only sleeping for four, five or six hours a night? Should you still aim to get up seven or eight hours after you go to bed?

If this is your situation it's best to take things gradually. The issue here is one of *sleep efficiency*, which is calculated by dividing the time you spend asleep by the time you spend in bed, and then multiplying by 100. So if you sleep for six hours but spend eight hours in bed your sleep efficiency is 75 per cent. Ideally we should be aiming for 85 per cent or above. If we're in bed, we want to be asleep and not tossing or turning or reading or watching the TV. Remember that we're teaching our mind and body that bed means one thing only: sleep.

If you're currently getting six hours sleep an efficiency of 85 per cent works out as seven hours in bed. So for now choose times that fit this scenario – bed at midnight and getting up at 7 a.m., for instance. Once you're sleeping better you can extend the time you spend in bed.

Some people find it helpful to aim for 100 per cent efficiency. Six hours sleep a night, for instance, means exactly six hours in bed. This technique is known as *sleep restriction* and again the idea is that as your sleep improves you can steadily increase the amount of time you spend in bed.

People who have fallen into the habit of going to bed in the early hours of the morning – what's known as *delayed sleep phase* – will need to tweak this technique a little. Changing an engrained sleep pattern overnight (so to speak) is a tough ask. So rather than suddenly switching your bedtime from 3 a.m. to 11 p.m., move it forward gradually in stages of twenty to thirty minutes a week.

If you've not fallen asleep within fifteen to twenty minutes, get out of bed. We're aiming to build an exclusive relationship between bed and sleep. Lying awake for ages is definitely off the agenda. So if you haven't fallen asleep twenty minutes after turning out the light – or if you've woken up in the night – it's best to get out of bed. Choose somewhere warm and not too brightly lit and let yourself relax; read a favourite book, perhaps, or meditate. When you feel drowsy you can head back to bed.

Only use your bed for sleep. Snuggling in bed can be so comfortable that it's tempting to base oneself there! The allure is even more compelling given that the Internet allows us to shop from bed, work from bed, socialise from bed, watch movies from bed, and so on. When we're sleeping well, none of this is a problem. But if insomnia has become an issue for us we need to get back to basics. It's that equation again: bed = sleep! (The only exception to this rule is sex and that's because it generally leaves people feeling drowsy.)

Don't nap in the daytime. Lovely though an afternoon snooze can be, napping isn't a good idea if we're sleeping poorly at night. Our insomnia may have left us feeling desperately tired, but by napping we risk sending both our sleep homeostat and our body clock awry.

Our homeostat, remember, takes its bearings from the last time we slept. If we've slept during the day we're unlikely to feel sleepy at bedtime. Our body clock, meanwhile, expects us to be awake during the day. (It's true that most of us experience a dip in energy levels in the afternoon and a nap at this time can be really refreshing. But until our night-time sleep is sorted out it's best avoided.)

Incidentally, if you're scheduled to do something potentially dangerous – driving long distances, for instance, or operating machinery – you're better off getting the sleep you need, even if it is during the day.

A word about sleeping pills and other remedies

When insomnia becomes really bad sleeping pills can seem highly attractive. And for a very short period, and to secure some much-needed rest, they can be a helpful option.

However, we don't recommend them as a long-term strategy. What happens is that our body becomes used to the drug, which means that we need a higher dose for the tablets to work. Sleeping pills can also be addictive; if you've been taking them for a while it can be tough to stop.

What about over-the-counter remedies? Some people find them helpful but again they're not a long-term solution to sleeplessness. Because they often contain antihistamines they can leave you feeling dopey the next day. And just like prescribed sleeping pills, some people find them addictive.

Some people swear by natural remedies such as valerian, chamomile and lavender. If they work for you, that's great. But convincing clinical evidence for their effectiveness is lacking. It's the same with warm milk: many people think it's a great solution to insomnia, but as yet we just don't know one way or another. That said, it's true that warm milk is rich in an amino acid called trytophan, which is a natural sedative. Adding honey, so the theory goes, helps the body to process the tryptophan more speedily.

Overcoming nightmares

For some people nightmares can have a hugely negative impact on their sleep, jolting them awake in the early hours and leaving them so upset that getting back to sleep quickly is extremely difficult. Some studies have suggested that 3 per cent of adults experience nightmares at least once a week.

Why nightmares happen is still a mystery. But we know they mostly occur in the comparatively light REM sleep. This final stage of the sleep cycle occurs throughout the night – as you may remember, we go through the cycle several times in a night – but it lasts longer towards morning, perhaps because the body is gradually gearing itself up to be awake.

What can we do to prevent nightmares occurring? Poor sleep can trigger them, so the first step is to put into practice the suggestions earlier in this chapter for improving sleep. Second, it may be that your nightmares are being caused by medication. Beta-blockers and the SSRI antidepressant paroxetine, for instance, have both been linked to bad dreams. So if you think this may be a factor in your nightmares do talk to your doctor.

The third remedy is a tried-and-tested technique called **imagery rehearsal**, which is designed to help people who regularly experience the same nightmare. All you need to do is retell the story of your nightmare, but this time with a happy ending. You can alter the dream any way you like; make whatever changes you feel will remove the fear or other negative emotions. Then spend a few minutes every day rehearsing this revised version in your mind. Gradually you'll discover that your nightmares have lost their power to distress you.

Sleep apnea

It's worth mentioning that breathing difficulties can be a factor in poor sleep. In sleep apnea the muscles and soft tissue in the back of the throat collapse inwards, restricting the airway. The oxygen supply to our body falls and our brain wakes us up so that we can breathe normally. This can happen dozens of times a night, leaving us exhausted the following morning.

We're at greater risk of sleep apnea if we're:

- male;
- overweight;
- have a thick neck;
- have been drinking or smoking.

Most people with sleep apnea don't remember these night-time incidents, though they're certainly aware of their sleepiness during the day. It's usually a bed partner who notices that all may not be quite right, perhaps because of heavy snoring or choking, snorting or gasping during sleep. Apnea is a serious condition, but specific treatments are available. If you think it may be an issue for you, ask your GP to organise a specialist sleep assessment.

Chapter summary

- Sleep problems tend to make suspicious thoughts worse, so it's sensible to sort them out now.
- Bring your sleep into harmony with your circadian rhythms: have a morning walk outside; avoid bright light at night; exercise every day; steer clear of caffeine, nicotine or alcohol in the evening; and develop a wind-down routine.

- Learn to associate your bed with sleep: go to bed and get up at the same times each day; avoid daytime naps; don't stay in bed if you're not sleeping; and use your bed only for sleep.

9

Boosting your self-confidence

Introduction

How many suspicious thoughts do you have when you're feeling really happy and self-confident? And if you do have them when you're feeling on top form, how much of an effect do they have on you?

The world looks different when we're feeling positive about ourselves. In fact, it doesn't just look different: it looks *better*. So we're much less likely to be suspicious of other people when our self-esteem is in good shape. If suspicious thoughts do pop up, the chances are we'll just ignore them.

When we're feeling negative about ourselves, on the other hand, we're much more likely to have problems with paranoid thoughts. Our sadness, anxiety or anger can foster a sense of vulnerability. We feel isolated and inferior, easy prey for the self-assured winners we seem to run into everywhere.

This is where the next two steps of the programme come in. If we can improve the way we feel about ourselves and the world, we'll reduce the number of paranoid thoughts we have. And because problems are far easier to deal with when we're feeling happy, we'll be in a much better position to cope with those thoughts if they do occur. Making this kind of change isn't always easy. As the psychologist Rick Hanson has pointed out, the human mind tends to function like Velcro for negative experiences but like Teflon for the positive in life. But we can learn to reverse that habit, and Steps 5 and 6 will show you how.

First let's spend a little time exploring why we might come to feel negative about ourselves, and the effects on our mood and behaviour.

What determines our level of self-esteem?

Where do our thoughts about ourselves – or our self-esteem – come from?

Self-esteem is principally the product of our life experiences: the way we were brought up; our position in society and in the various groups we belong to (our families or school class, for instance); our interactions with other people; and the things that have happened to us. Our genes can be a factor too, though a less important one.

Given the sheer number of influences involved, it's not surprising that self-esteem is a complex phenomenon. It's generally not possible to point to a single event in order to explain our self-esteem: it's the product of a combination of factors, and it often changes over time.

That said it's normally true that bad experiences lower our self-esteem and good ones raise it. If you think about your own life, you'll probably find that it's when unpleasant things have happened that you feel negative about yourself. The curve balls life sometimes throws at us can smash right through our self-esteem. This is understandable – but it isn't inevitable.

The vicious cycle of negative thoughts, low mood and reinforcing behaviour

When you hear the word 'mood' you probably associate it with feelings. And you'd be right to do so. But our moods are hugely influenced by our thoughts, and particularly thoughts about ourselves. Negative thoughts – unsurprisingly – lead to negative moods. Unfortunately, negative moods tend to make our thoughts even darker. And this can easily lead to changes in our behaviour, when we withdraw, give up too easily, or simply send the wrong signals to others. Let's look at this vicious cycle more closely.

Throughout this book we draw on the pioneering psychological research of **cognitive behavioural therapy** (CBT). CBT was originally developed to help people deal with low mood – by which we mean feeling down or depressed or sad or anxious or worried. The American psychiatrist Dr Aaron Beck is one of the founders of CBT and his work has given us really important insights into the causes of low mood. Basically, our moods are the product of:

- Our thoughts;
- Our thinking style;
- Our behaviour.

Our thoughts

It seems reasonable to assume that it's what happens to us in our life that leads directly to how we feel. We can capture this in a little diagram:

Events →→→ Feelings

After all, if we're going through a rough patch in a relationship or have lost our job, for instance, we're naturally going to feel down, aren't we?

Well, not necessarily. More often than not it's the way we *think about* those events that determines how we're going to feel. Take, for instance, a group of people who've all been made redundant by the same employer. Their reactions to this apparently negative event may well be very different.

One person might think: 'Fantastic. I should have made a move by now anyway. This is the kick up the backside I need to get on and do what I really want to with my career.' This person probably feels happy. Another might take a philosophical view of events: 'It's a shame, but these things happen. I knew the company was struggling so I wasn't surprised. I'll find something else and I've got the redundancy package to help me until I do.'

For someone else, being laid off is much more traumatic: 'I knew they wanted to get rid of me. This is just the excuse they've been waiting for. It's how they always get shot of people they don't rate. What on earth am I going to do now?' This person probably feels miserable. Now, as you've doubtless noticed, this person has some pretty negative thoughts about themselves. And those thoughts will surely have influenced their mood.

We can't predict how someone is going to feel just by looking at what's happened to him or her. To know how they feel, we have to know *what they're thinking*. As the poet John Milton wrote: 'The mind is its own place, and in itself can make a Heaven of Hell, a Hell of Heaven.' So we need to make a change to our diagram:

Events →→→ Thoughts →→→ Feelings

Events cause us to think certain thoughts that in turn produce particular feelings. And *negative thoughts produce negative feelings: they make us unhappy*. On the other hand, *thinking positively will help us feel happier*. You can see how much is at stake in changing the way we think about the stuff that happens to us!

Our thinking style

Thinking is the way we make sense of the world and our

experiences. It's hugely influenced by our mood, but it also then *reinforces* our mood, as we'll see below. When we're feeling down, the way we think may well be affected in one or more of the following ways:

- **All or nothing thinking** Things can look very black and white when we're not feeling great. Life is either great or terrible; we're either a total success or a complete failure. If we're feeling down, we'll probably see life as terrible and ourselves as a failure. We don't tend to be very interested in a more balanced view of the situation: it's all or nothing.
- **Ignoring the positive** It's hard to see the good things when our mood is low. We focus on all the bad stuff and anything else is either invisible to us or insignificant. For example, if someone praises us for a piece of work we've done, we'll probably decide that they're just being polite or that they've not noticed the problems in our work. It's the belief confirmation bias all over again (see pages 121–123 for more on this). Research has shown that our mood affects our *memory*: when we're down, we actually find it much easier to remember negative experiences than we do positive ones.
- **Taking things personally** When we're feeling down it can seem as if every little event is

> a result of something we've done. If someone moves away from us on the bus it's because they don't like the way we look (and not because they want to have a seat to themselves). If our boss is grumpy in a Monday morning meeting it's because we've done something to annoy them (and not because she slept badly the night before or has had a stressful weekend). We don't think through *alternative explanations* (see pages 121–125): we just assume that we're the problem.

Our mood is hardly likely to improve when we're thinking like this. It's as if we're seeing the world through very badly focused glasses!

Our behaviour

Have a look back at the stories of Keith and Emily in Chapter 4. Their suspicious thoughts ended up making them feel so low that neither of them wanted to leave the house. Social contact – whether it was going to work or seeing friends – seemed too stressful. They did less and less, retreating into their homes and channelling all their energy into worrying.

Keith and Emily's cases show the way our behaviour and our mood are interconnected. When we're happy, we're likely to be out and about, busy with work and hobbies and family and friends. And these are just the sort of behaviours and experiences that will keep our good mood going.

When we're feeling down, on the other hand, we're much more likely to do less. All of the activities that we used to do – including the ones we really enjoyed – now seem too difficult to face. Unfortunately, all this does is make us feel even more miserable and even less like doing things. After all, what we've done is remove from our lives the things that give us pleasure and a sense of achievement. Instead of feeling alive and involved in the world, we feel isolated and abandoned. Small wonder we feel even lower than we did before.

So how do we break the vicious cycle? How do we ensure that the way we think *raises* our mood and *boosts* our level of activity? Because if we can do that, we'll be well on the way to overcoming our suspicious thoughts.

Step 5 Increase your self-confidence

A fantastic counterweight to negative thoughts is having an accessible and richly developed positive view of ourselves – what we might think of as *self-confidence.*

Finding the meaning

Psychologists have done a lot of research in recent years into happiness. They've found that one of the hallmarks of contented, self-confident people is that they have managed to fill their lives with *meaning*. Where they find that meaning is a very individual thing. For some people it's work; for others family; and for others still religion, political activism, sport or a hobby. The activity itself doesn't matter: what's important here is the *effect* on our mood. (Of course, there's no reason why you shouldn't find meaning in a variety of activities.)

If you feel as though your life lacks that sense of meaning, spend a little time reflecting on what's important to you. What activity would engage you? What would give you a sense of achievement and pride? What would help you feel more positive about yourself?

Perhaps you're struggling for ideas. So think back over the years: what's worked for you in the past? Perhaps it's something that's been crowded out as life has become more complex. Or ask yourself: how would I like people to think of me? As a true friend, perhaps. Or a passionate campaigner for a cause. A dedicated, loving parent or a determined, hard-working professional. Who do you admire – and how could you be more like them?

When you have your answer – and if you're not sure, try a range of possibilities – the trick is simply to make sure that you give that activity the time it merits. Keep a diary and *schedule it in*. Don't let other commitments edge it out. After all, what could be more important than feeling better about yourself?

Now let's look at three exercises that are specifically designed to boost our self-confidence.

Exercise A: Get your five a day!

It can sometimes appear as if self-confidence is something we're simply born with – or without. Similarly, it can seem to wax and wane as events befall us. But we can influence our level of self-confidence. One very effective way of doing that is through the activities we choose.

So here are your 'five a day' for well-being, as recommended by the UK government's panel of expert advisers:

- **Connect** The quality of our relationships is a huge influence on our happiness and self-confidence. Make time for the important people in your life – your family and friends, colleagues and neighbours.
- **Be active** It's easy to forget that our minds and bodies are interconnected. But it becomes obvious when we exercise: our body thrives on physical activity, but so too does our mind. Aim for at least thirty minutes of exercise several times a week. If you're starting from zero, you may prefer to begin with every other day and build up from there.
- **Be curious** Psychologists have noted – and you may well have done so too – that happy people tend to also be *curious* people: life intrigues them. So cultivate your curiosity. Take a few moments to notice what's going on around you. Savour

the colours and sounds and movement. What is the most appealing thing you can see? What is the most mysterious? What would you like to know more about?

- **Learn** This may not tally with your experience of school, but learning is great for our mental health! Whether it's a new language, a dance step or a DIY task, the sense of engagement and achievement that comes when we're learning something new is a real boost.
- **Give** Helping others – giving our time, attention and energy – is a crucial element of well-being. When researchers in Germany followed the fortunes of thousands of people over several years they found that those who were committed to helping other people were significantly happier – as were those who prioritised family, friends and social and political activities. When we think about it, that's not surprising: what better way is there to make a positive difference in our lives?

How are you doing on your five a day right now? If you think you could add more of these activities to your week, we recommend you plan them into your diary. Free time may be scarce for you. If so, take it gradually. Add one target activity to your week: a few minutes a day, or an hour or two a week, is fine to begin with. For example, if you notice you're not as physically active as you'd like, try a brisk twenty-minute walk each day or a weekly swim.

If you're finding it hard to think of a positive activity that's right for you, ask yourself the following questions:

- *What could I do for an afternoon that I'd find really enjoyable or satisfying?*
- *What could I do for an hour?*
- *Is there something good I could plan to do one weekend?*
- *What can I do that costs money?*
- *What can I do for free?*
- *What could I do that will really stimulate my mind?*
- *What would give me a sense of achievement?*
- *Is there a course or evening class I'd find interesting?*
- *What physical activity would I like to do?*
- *What about learning some practical skill?*
- *If a friend was visiting, what would I suggest we do?*
- *Do I want to meet new people?*
- *Do I want to make new friends?*
- *What enjoyable activity could I do on my own?*
- *What could I do at home?*
- *Where would I like to go?*

- *What could I do that I've never done before?*
- *What have I enjoyed doing in the past?*
- *Are there any interesting events or activities listed in the paper?*
- *How about voluntary work?*

Exercise B: Remember your strengths

Many of us find it much easier to think of our weaknesses than we do our strengths. We may see plenty of great attributes in the people around us, but we underestimate ourselves. If we're feeling really low, it may seem like we have nothing at all to be proud of – which of course only reinforces our negative mood.

This exercise is designed to help you perceive the positive qualities that – whether you're aware of them or not – you most definitely possess. So, right now, jot down a list of your strengths.

How many did you think of? Whatever the number, we're willing to bet that you've missed a few. Which of the following list, devised by the Values in Action Institute, could you apply to yourself?

Creativity	Curiosity
Love of learning	Open-mindedness
Perspective	Authenticity/genuineness/honesty
Bravery	Persistence
Zest/energy/wholeheartedness	Kindness
Love	Social intelligence (being sensitive to other people's needs and desires)
Fairness	Leadership
Teamwork	Forgiveness/mercy
Modesty/humility	Prudence
Self-discipline	Appreciation of beauty and excellence
Gratitude	Hope
Humour	Religiousness/spirituality

From http://www.viacharacter.org/www/Character-Strengths/VIA-Classification

Experts have suggested that, to become happier, we should aim to fill our lives with activities that build on our natural strengths. When you've identified yours, aim to add in activities that do just that. If you're creative, for example, look for new ways to use that strength. If spiritual matters intrigue you, consider what you can do to develop that interest. And if you're never happier than when researching a new subject make learning a core part of your life.

Exercise C: Shifting your focus to the positive

You'll probably have noticed that our moods can often be all-pervasive: they influence everything we do, say, think and feel. This means that when we're feeling low we tend only to notice the negative things in life – the things that confirm our dark mood. But if we can shift our focus on to the good stuff, we can give our sense of well-being a real lift. To help you, here are three much-used techniques. Choose one that appeals to you and give it a go for a week. If you find it helpful, build it into your routine. Feel free to try all three if you fancy (though probably not at the same time).

Record the positives This is another exercise that requires the use of a diary. For seven days keep a note of the good things that happen to you and how they made you feel. You may want to use this format:

Day	Positive thing	How do I feel?

It may seem as though nothing really great happens: you didn't win the lottery, or land your dream job, or discover a long-lost friend. But of course if any of those happened we wouldn't need a diary to notice them! What we want you to focus on are the details, the things that might seem pretty insignificant but in fact are brilliant little morale-boosters: a delicious meal, a walk in the sunshine, a chat with someone you care about, a TV programme you've enjoyed. These are the 'nuts and bolts' of well-being. When you review your diary at the end of the week, you'll see that you're much richer in them than you think.

Find three positive things in each day Every evening – perhaps as you're preparing for bed – think back over your day. What three good things happened? As with the previous exercise, the trick here is to notice the details!

Savour the moment Most of us aren't especially good at living in the moment. Our minds are constantly turning back to past events or thinking about the future. And that means we risk overlooking the contentment that can visit us at any moment.

So pause, look around you, and ask yourself: *What is going right for me right now?* If it's tricky to think of anything good, try to keep going until you have at least one positive.

Here's an example:

- Beautiful weather outside.
- Feeling rested and healthy.
- Got some work done this morning.

- Cat dozing on nearby chair.
- Looking forward to mid-morning cup of coffee!

There are two really nice things about this particular activity. First is the fact that spending just a few moments focusing on the positive things in your current situation boosts your mood. Secondly, identifying what's good in your life allows you to seek more of it. For example, though there's not much we can do about the weather, we can note our satisfaction at a productive morning's work and aim to reproduce that feeling as often as possible.

What this exercise shows us is how to recognise and *savour* the good things in life, no matter how small. By savouring we mean taking the time to notice, and delight in, an experience – to really kick back and bask in the pleasure of the moment, and to try to make that pleasure *last*.

There are other, very simple ways of doing this. For example, we can take a little time each day to really focus on what we're doing and how we're feeling. Give it a go when, for instance, you next eat a piece of fruit; spend time with friends; finish a piece of work you're pleased with; or simply breathe the fresh air outside.

Try to take in every detail of the moment; revel in your enjoyment. What are your senses telling you? Focus on the precise taste of the fruit; feel the breeze play across your face; listen intently to your friends' voices. Give yourself up to the moment; aim to inhabit it with your whole spirit.

Savouring isn't merely something we can do in the present. We can savour the future and the past too. Whether it's a holiday you've just booked, a meal you're cooking for friends, a walk in the countryside, a massage or a trip to buy new clothes, spend a few minutes each day actively looking forward to these treats. Allow yourself the luxury of a daydream, especially if you're feeling low: thinking about future fun is sure to pick you up.

Even when the event you've looked forward to is over, it can still be a great source of pleasure. Make the effort to remember what happened and relish every little detail. Take photos. Relive the moment by reminiscing with friends. Perhaps write a brief note of what happened and, in particular, how much happiness it gave you.

If you can savour an experience beforehand, while it's happening and afterwards, think how far you're making that pleasure go!

Happy memories make a brilliant pick-me-up. A nice idea suggested by the psychologist Sonia Lyubomirsky is to create a 'savouring album'. Fill it with photos and other mementoes of all that is dearest to you in life – perhaps your friends, partner, children, pet, home or souvenirs from a special holiday. Don't bury the album away in a drawer. Keep it somewhere accessible. Perhaps, as Lyubomirsky does, take it with you when you travel. That way, it'll always be on hand when you need a lift.

Step 6 Decreasing negative thoughts about yourself

The techniques we've set out in Step 5 will help you become more attuned to your positive thoughts – which in turn will lessen the impact of the more negative thoughts.

But of course negative thoughts are unlikely to disappear overnight. If we're prone to paranoia we may well have a pretty low opinion of ourselves. We may think of ourselves as: *unlikeable, inferior, incompetent, weak, foolish, different, odd, unattractive, worthless, bad, unloved, unpopular.* These kinds of thoughts can leave us feeling alone and vulnerable, which we know provides fertile ground for paranoia. (Actually, it's worth remembering that a surprisingly high proportion of people who *don't* experience suspicious thoughts feel this negatively about themselves.)

What can we do to tackle thoughts like this head on? The remainder of this chapter will show you.

Exercise A: Put your negative thoughts to the test

The psychologist Paul Gilbert has coined the phrase 'inner compassion'. He points out that many of us are often wonderfully supportive, sympathetic and sensitive towards other people, but much less likely to show that level of compassion when it comes to judging ourselves. We demand far more of ourselves than we do of others – and we're incredibly hard on ourselves when we don't live up to our impossibly high standards.

This next exercise provides an opportunity to practise cultivating your inner compassion. First, write down a negative thought about yourself – one that you can remember thinking on a specific recent occasion. Rate how strongly you believe that thought on a scale of 0 to 100 per cent.

Now jot down the evidence for and against the thought. Why should you believe it? If you wanted to justify it to someone else, what reasons would you give? Why might that thought be wrong? What would you tell a friend who expressed a thought like this about themselves?

Once you've considered the evidence, re-rate the strength of your belief in the thought. As you do so, remember to use your inner compassion. Go easy on yourself.

The next stage is to test your negative thought. Instead of simply carrying it around in your mind, get it out into the light of day – and then see how convincing it looks. For example, if you're worried that you're unlikeable, arrange to spend more time with the people you know. If you believe you're worthless, organise some activities that will give you a sense of meaning: help a friend or family member, perhaps, or volunteer your time for a good cause.

Once you've tested your thought, ask yourself how strongly you believe it now. We're willing to bet that – with the help of a little inner compassion – it'll seem much less convincing.

Exercise B: Positive imagery

It's easy to forget that many of our thoughts aren't expressed in words but in *images*. There's something about imagery – a directness, perhaps – that makes it particularly influential for our emotions. Mental images both express our emotions and reinforce them.

Negative images can be especially powerful. They're also common: most people have experienced them at one time or another, and perhaps you have too. We see ourselves messing up. We look foolish – ridiculous. Our failings are so obvious that it's no wonder other people view us with contempt or hostility.

Positive images, on the other hand, seem to come less easily to many of us. What would we look like if we were succeeding? We don't know.

So let's explore some ways in which we can:

- Deprive negative images of their power over us;
- Learn to visualise success.

Let's tackle those negative images first. One very effective technique is simply to *let them go*. This means that we don't try to suppress or fight the image. We don't pretend that it hasn't come into our mind. We acknowledge it. We might say to ourselves: 'Ah, there's that image again of me . . .'. But we don't waste time thinking about it. We don't attach any importance to it. We maintain our focus on what we're doing. And soon enough the image will fade into oblivion – just like the thousands of other thoughts we've had that day.

Another technique is to *re-work* the image. Choose one that's been bothering you lately. And then, in your imagination, change it in any way that takes your fancy. In negative images we generally see ourselves from the perspective of another person. We are passive; trapped in the picture. But it's only a picture; it definitely isn't reality. And we can alter it however we choose.

Try removing the negative parts of the image, as if you were taking an eraser to a sketch. Or pick up your imaginary pencil and add in some positive elements. Using humour can be a really effective way of undermining a negative image: if you can make yourself smile you're definitely on the right track. You might like to run the image on as if it were a frame from a movie – but one with a happy ending!

Take the time to really familiarise yourself with the reworked imagery. Let it take root in your memory. And if the upsetting image should make another appearance, you'll be ready for it.

Now let's turn to **visualising success**. This is a technique used all the time in sports. In negative imagery we tend to see ourselves from the outside. But here we're looking through our own eyes. We're active, not passive. As British Olympic gold medallist Jessica Ennis has explained:

> *I use a lot of visualisation. I visualise the whole heptathlon a day before, two days before I compete and also*

> *during the event as well. It allows me to go through the perfect motion of what I want to achieve from each event. And it gives me a really positive outlook before I go out and compete.*
>
> (Source: http://www.youtube.com/watch?v=2APYZoezsjM)

Choose a situation that makes you anxious or fearful (speaking in public, perhaps, or walking through a busy shopping street) and then imagine that things go as well as they possibly could. In your mind's eye, you've aced it – and it feels great. Positive energy floods through you. You are calm, self-assured, impressive.

Spend a few minutes each day visualising success. You'll feel your self-confidence gradually grow. And use the technique before you go into the sort of situations that worry you. Just like Jessica Ennis, you'll find that it's a great preparation for success.

Exercise C: Change the goals

As we've seen, we human beings have a tendency to look for confirmation of what we already think we know. And it can take an awful lot of very hard evidence to change our minds!

One of the problems with this way of thinking is that it can generate unhelpful expectations. For example, if we go into a social situation expecting to make a fool of ourselves, or we try to build a friendship while expecting rejection, then we're already on the lookout for disaster. What could be a positive experience becomes a damage-limitation exercise.

So ask yourself:

- What is your positive goal in the situations that tend to trigger negative thoughts?
- What would you like to achieve?
- What would give you pleasure?

Rather than your worries, aim to make these positive objectives the focus of your attention. And because our minds find it more or less impossible to think two contradictory thoughts, you'll discover that your negative expectations recede. You'll be calmer, more optimistic and in a much better position to cope with stressful situations.

To break the negative focus of attention underpinning our negative thoughts, we need to view things differently. We need to direct our thoughts away from what we fear and towards the positive.

Changing your goals is one way to do this. Another, closely related technique is to capitalise on your interests and strengths – to use them to help you look at the situations that trigger your anxiety from a more optimistic perspective.

We recently came across a fantastic illustration of this technique. Lucy sought out the help of a therapist because of problems at work. She believed that her colleagues were all more intelligent, and better at their jobs, than she was.

With such a low opinion of herself, talking to colleagues could be a very stressful experience.

In particular, the many social occasions organised by the company had become a nightmare for her. As each approached, Lucy's anxiety would increase. Convinced that her colleagues must look down on her, and that every time she opened her mouth she'd show why they were right to do so, she would hover on the margins, doing her best to avoid being drawn into a conversation, and constantly checking her watch to find out how much more she would have to endure. Many of Lucy's colleagues assumed that she preferred her own company and left her to it – which only reinforced Lucy's belief that they didn't like her.

In the course of one of their chats, the therapist had discovered that Lucy was an avid bird-watcher. So he suggested that she apply her ornithological skills to the social occasions that made her so anxious. He wasn't, of course, asking her to spend the evening scanning the room for peregrine falcons. Not literally, anyway. What he had in mind was that she should imagine the people around her as birds. When she observed them carefully, which birds did they most remind her of? Who was a sparrow and who was an eagle? Who were the songbirds and who was more like the chattering jackdaw? Who were the brightly coloured parakeets and birds of paradise?

The idea worked brilliantly. It switched Lucy's attention away from her own imagined failings and redirected it outwards towards the people she was with. But when she looked at her colleagues, it wasn't in order to confirm her fears. Instead she was observing them from a completely different perspective – and, because bird-watching was a source of so much pleasure for her, it was a perspective that had only positive associations. Suddenly, she felt in control of the situation. Her anxiety receded. And she found it far easier to chat to her colleagues.

Could you apply this technique to your own negative thoughts? Can you think of ways in which you can use your interests and strengths to help shift your focus of attention? Maybe you're a keen reader, or you love movies. Perhaps you're really into clothes, or music. When you find yourself in a situation that makes you anxious, you could concentrate on what people are wearing, or which characters they remind you of, or which piece of music would best suit a soundtrack for the scene.

Sceptical? Wondering whether this could work for you? Well, why not conduct an experiment. The next time you're anxious about something, focus on the negative aspects of the situation. Let your fear determine your goals, so that your objective is simply to avoid harm. On the occasion after that, try switching your attention to the positive. Then ask yourself: which worked best? Was shifting your attention helpful? Did it lower your anxiety? Did it make it easier for you to cope?

Learning to be more assertive

When our self-esteem is low, or when we're feeling down, we're often very reluctant to tell people what we want or need. Instead of expressing our feelings – for example, if someone's done something to upset us – we tend to shrink into the background and 'go with the flow'.

This *timidity* (or passiveness) stems from our fear about what might happen if we *do* express ourselves. Maybe we'll get into an argument, or the other person will think we're stupid. Maybe they'll just take no notice of us. If we say nothing, we'll avoid any unpleasant confrontation, won't we?

Well, avoiding confrontation can make us feel better in the short term. But the long-term consequences of timidity aren't so good. We come to see ourselves as weak and passive, always doing what other people want and never having the courage to stand up for our own needs and desires. Our self-esteem takes a real hit, and we can also feel a lot of resentment towards other people. So timidity makes us feel bad both about ourselves and the people around us. We're also not being fair: other people have a right to know if they're upsetting or annoying us.

So we need to ditch our timidity and replace it with *assertiveness*. Assertiveness is really a recognition that other people aren't mind-readers! No one can know what we're thinking unless we tell him or her. So we need to *express ourselves* and let the people around us know how we feel and what we want. If you're not an assertive person right now, it can be hard to imagine that you ever will be. But assertiveness can definitely be learned, and we'll give you some pointers in the next couple of pages.

By the way, assertiveness is sometimes confused with aggression. But it's not about getting what we want at all costs. We need to *respect* other people's feelings and remember that they, just like us, have needs and desires that deserve a fair hearing.

Okay, how do we go about being assertive? The first step is to be clear about what we want. If someone at work is making a joke at your expense, for example, you need to decide what you want to happen. Are you happy to let it go, or do you want this kind of thing to stop?

Let's say you've decided you want the joking to stop – what do you do next? Well, you need to tell the person concerned how you feel and what you want. Try to stay as cool and matter-of-fact as possible – in fact, if you've been really upset or angered by something that's happened, it's a good idea to wait until you're feeling calmer before you have this conversation.

Make it very clear how you feel, but don't use extreme language like 'you always . . .' or 'you never . . .'. Just concentrate on the incident at hand. Focus on the *effect* of the other person's behaviour rather than what they may have been intending to achieve. We can't know for sure that the person meant to upset us by telling that joke. But we do know how it made us feel – and that's what we should be explaining to them. So you might say something like, 'I'm sure you didn't mean to, but that joke really upset me.'

Once you've communicated how you feel, move on to what you want to happen. Again, make it as clear – and specific – as you can. Don't say you don't want them to upset you again: that's too vague. Tell them, 'I'd appreciate it if you didn't make these kinds of jokes about me in the future.'

Try to stay as calm and friendly as you can. No one responds positively when they feel they're under attack. If you go in all guns blazing, you'll probably just end up in a row. Bear in mind that most of us are very bad at judging how other people see our behaviour. You might well find that the person who made the joke had no idea of the effect it would have on you. They weren't being malicious, only thoughtless. And if you get a constructive response to your comments, remember to thank the other person for it.

One area where lots of us find it especially difficult to express our feelings is when we're asked to do something. We've all found ourselves loaded down with jobs we've no time or inclination to do simply because we find it impossible to say 'No'. Sometimes it's because we just want to be helpful. Sometimes it's because we're too scared of the consequences to say what we really think. Either way, not being able to say 'No' isn't going to do much for our self-esteem. You can imagine how we'll feel about ourselves if the only thing preventing us from saying 'No' is fear. But even if we start out feeling good about ourselves for being so obliging, we'll probably end up feeling like we're really just too timid to stand up for ourselves.

So here are some techniques you can use to help you with that tiny but ever so tricky word!

- Buy yourself the time you need to be assertive (or if you're not sure how you feel about a task).

When someone asks you to do something, tell them you'll think about it.

- Don't make excuses and don't give reasons: just say no. For example, you could say 'No, I am sorry but I can't' or 'No, I can't do it this time' or just 'No, I'm sorry'. This is called the 'broken record' technique and is especially good for those situations where you're absolutely sure you don't want to do what you've been asked. Keeping it this short and sweet is a reflection of the fact that you don't need permission for your decision. You don't have to persuade anyone that your decision is the right one – except perhaps yourself!
- Sometimes you'll want to show you appreciate being asked even though you're not able to help. So you might say, 'It's kind of you to ask me, but I can't' or 'Thanks for thinking of me, but I'd rather not'.
- Be sympathetic and constructive. Tell the person you see their problem and help them think through possible solutions – as long as they don't involve you, of course!
- Explain why you can't help. But don't fall into the trap of sounding as if you're making excuses. Remember: you have a valid reason for your decision and you don't need anyone's approval.

- Sometimes you might want to meet the other person halfway: 'I can't do X, but I may be able to help you with Y.'

If you know you find it hard to be assertive in certain situations, it's a good idea to plan ahead. Think of all the ways you could react in the future and then weigh up their pros and cons. Once you've decided on the best approach, think through what you'd say. Visualise the situation as clearly as you can and rehearse your lines until you know them by heart. The more practice you do, the easier it'll get. That said, we know that learning to be assertive can be hard, at least at first. It takes courage to speak up for yourself – and you should remember that when you do! Give yourself the praise you deserve.

Building up friendships

You may not be astonished to learn that research has shown that friendships make a huge difference to our happiness and self-esteem.

This doesn't mean that we can't be content without dozens of friends and a hectic social life. Far from it. Quality is definitely more important than quantity. A few close friends – and in particular a best friend – will do the job perfectly.

But how do we build and maintain close friendships? What makes close relationships work? When psychologists asked people in the UK, Italy, Hong Kong and Japan to list the components of a successful friendship, here's what they came up with:

The rules of friendship

- Volunteer help in time of need.
- Respect the other person's privacy.
- Keep confidences.
- Trust and confide in each other.
- Stand up for the other person in their absence.
- Don't criticise each other in public.
- Show emotional support.
- Look him/her in the eye during conversations.
- Strive to make him/her happy while in each other's company.
- Don't be jealous or critical of each other's relationships.
- Be tolerant of each other's friends.
- Share news of success with the other person.
- Ask for personal advice.
- Don't nag.
- Engage in joking or teasing with the friend.
- Seek to repay debts and favours and compliments.
- Disclose personal feelings or problems to the friend.

Think about your own friendships. What makes them flourish? What could you do to strengthen them? Building on the rules of friendship, here are five key techniques for a better relationship:

Express your gratitude Everyone enjoys being thanked (provided it's genuine), so when your friend does something to please you make sure you express your gratitude. A brief text message after a fun time with each other works wonders!

Make praise a habit When was the last time you praised a friend? Many of us find giving praise awkward, which is a shame since reciprocal praise and admiration can really help friendships to blossom. Steer clear of empty flattery, but let your friend know how highly you think of them.

Remember what makes your friend special It's great, of course, to be able to rely on a friend. But when we feel secure in a relationship there's a risk that we'll start to take the other person for granted – that we'll forget how fortunate we are to have them around. So jot down three things (or more) that you particularly like about your friend. What is it about their personality that you value? What talents do they possess? And how have they displayed these positive traits lately?

Be helpful This one may seem like a no-brainer! On the other hand, life can be so hectic that being there for our friends can sometimes be tricky. So have a think: what could you do to help a friend? And then go ahead and do it!

Respond positively to good news The strongest relationships are built on what's called an 'active and constructive' response to good news. That means listening attentively, maintaining eye contact, and generally being as positive about the news – whether it's the big stuff or what seems like a minor event – as our friend is. By reacting like this we demonstrate how much we value our friend's happiness. We show that their pleasure gives us pleasure. And we thereby reinforce the bond between us.

Chapter summary

- By improving the way we feel about ourselves and the world, we'll reduce the number of paranoid thoughts we have.
- We can do this by:
    - Boosting our self-confidence;
    - Learning to cope with negative thoughts about ourselves;
    - Becoming more assertive;
    - Strengthening our friendships.

10

Learning safety: reviewing our paranoid and suspicious thoughts

Introduction

Suspicious thoughts don't just come to us out of the blue. They are our attempt to make sense of our experiences.

The world around us, and even the way we feel inside, can sometimes seem pretty mysterious. When it comes down to it, it's often very hard to be sure what our experiences really mean. Perhaps because it is so difficult we tend to interpret the present by looking back to the past. So when something happens to us, we remember similar experiences that we've had. This is perfectly natural: we use the knowledge we've gained over the course of our lives to help us in the present.

There's a drawback, though. If we're not careful our past experiences can get in the way of us seeing what's really going on in the here and now. We develop **preconceptions** about the world and don't stop to consider how accurate they are.

This can be a particular problem if we're prone to suspicious thoughts. If we've had negative experiences in the past – being bullied, for instance – we may well worry that other people will behave in the same way towards us in the future. If we're used to seeing other people as a threat, it's hard to break out of that mindset.

So we need to *slow down our thinking*, step back a little and make a conscious attempt to shake up our preconceptions. Don't let your reactions to your experiences become set in stone: *review them, challenge them*! Even if your views were right in the past they may not be right now.

This chapter is all about *testing* our preconceptions. We want you to reassess the way you make sense of your experiences. Challenging the way we think is hard; it can be like trying to unlearn a reflex. But you can definitely do it! You'll find it easier to do when you're calm – you'll not be in the mood to reassess anything if you're feeling really stressed or upset. This is what the exercises in the previous four chapters are designed to help you achieve. The knowledge you've gained about how and why your suspicious thoughts occur will also be a big help. And so too will the techniques and exercises we set out in this chapter.

When we test our suspicious thoughts we give ourselves the opportunity to discover whether we're safer than we fear. That's an extraordinarily important step. Because when we relearn safety – when we discover that the danger we dread isn't likely to occur – paranoia begins to melt away.

The rules of good decision-making

As we know, suspicious thoughts are a normal part of life: we all have them. After all, we have a lot of ambiguous information to make sense of: for example, the look on someone's face, a comment we overhear, or perhaps seeing the same car several times behind us on a journey.

It's our *reaction* to these thoughts that makes the difference. We have to decide how seriously to take them, and that decision can be crucial. When we're feeling down or anxious or stressed it's all too easy to jump to conclusions and assume the worst. But we need to treat these kinds of thoughts with real caution.

We can help ourselves to make good decisions about them by following these five rules:

- Don't treat thoughts and feelings as facts.
- Think of the evidence both for and against a thought.
- Always try to think of alternative explanations for an event.
- Test out your explanations.
- Keep an open mind.

Let's look at each of these rules in a little more detail.

Don't treat thoughts and feelings as facts

Scientific research has shown something very important about the way we think and make decisions: we rarely do it logically!

Our thoughts tend to come to us very quickly – so quickly, in fact, that it feels as if they're happening automatically. They're not based on what psychologists would call logical reasoning. They are not the product of careful consideration, rigorous testing and thorough review. Instead they're usually rooted in guesswork, feelings and intuition.

This is fair enough. After all, we have thousands of thoughts each day, most of which come and go without making much of an impression on us. It's hardly surprising that they're rather more haphazard than they are logical. But it does mean that we shouldn't treat them as if they were facts or truths. Most of our thoughts are just a snap reaction to what we see or feel.

It's the same with our feelings: we can't rely on them to give us an accurate picture of the world. Just because we *feel* threatened doesn't mean that we are. Making judgements and decisions on the basis of feelings is a risky strategy.

When you have a thought or feeling about something that happens to you, don't assume it's correct. It might be, but it might be wrong. Or it might be half-right. To find out which it is, we need to apply some logical reasoning. Learn how to do this by studying the next four rules of good decision-making!

Think of evidence both for and against a thought

We saw in Chapter 5 that once we start to believe a thought is true we notice all the evidence that seems to support it and none that doesn't. This is what psychologists call the **belief confirmation bias** and it explains why, in her lowest moments, Emily would focus only on the parts of her evening out that she saw as proving that her colleagues had a low opinion of her. Those details might be one overheard comment or one glance in her direction. The rest of the evening, which she might have spent chatting happily with people, meant nothing to her. For Emily, that good stuff was so insignificant it might as well not have happened at all.

Before you decide that a suspicious thought is true, *weigh the evidence.* We need to consider both the evidence that supports our thought *and* the evidence that doesn't. So if Emily sees a senior colleague look across the room at her, with what might have been a frown on his face, she has two sets of evidence to consider. On the one hand is her sense that the colleague really was frowning at her and the view held by several people in her firm that he has a low opinion of relatively young women lawyers. This might mean that he's thinking negative thoughts about Emily; this might be typical of the way *all* the senior partners in the firm think about her.

On the other hand, Emily needs to think through the possibility that her colleague may not have been looking at her and that, even if he was, he may not actually have been *thinking* about her. He might have been thinking of a thousand and one other things, or he might have been lost in a daydream. In any case, perhaps his eyesight isn't good enough to pick her out in a darkened room. Emily might also remember that she actually worked on a case with this man a year ago – and she found him perfectly friendly. It's possible, then, that the gossip in the office about his views on women lawyers is wrong. As for the other senior partners in the firm, Emily has had a friendly working relationship with some, a less positive experience with a couple of others, and hasn't worked at all with most of them. It'd be hard for her to come to any firm conclusions about how they all view her.

Once we spend a little time thinking through the evidence for a thought, we generally find that our first reaction to a situation isn't completely correct. We get a much more balanced perspective when we consider *both sides of the argument*. And with a balanced perspective, we're in a much better position to reach an accurate understanding of what we've been experiencing.

Always try to think of alternative explanations for an event

As part of our effort to weigh the evidence, we need to consider whether there are *alternative explanations* for the event that's prompted our suspicious thought. There are almost always lots of potential explanations for any occurrence, as the example we've just discussed involving Emily shows. We only have to take the time to think them through.

It's very important that we do consider the options in this way because the explanation we choose has such a big effect on the way we feel. If Emily thinks her colleague is frowning at her, it fuels her sense of being undervalued at work. On the other hand, if she decides he probably wasn't looking at her she's likely to feel a lot better about herself and her colleagues.

Test out your explanations

Let's recap for a moment. The things that happen to us in life prompt all kinds of off-the-cuff thoughts and feelings. Before we set too much store by these first reactions, we need to step back and think them through. Let's try to imagine all the possible explanations and consider the evidence to decide which is most likely to be true.

We can do more than just *think about* these possibilities: we can actually *test* them. Psychologists call it **reality testing**. For example, you might not have seen some old friends for several months and be worrying that they're avoiding you for some reason. One possible explanation is that you've accidentally upset them and so they are indeed keeping their distance. Another explanation is that they've been going through some tough times and are keeping themselves to themselves. And a third might be that you've all been really busy with work and other commitments and that your friends would love to see you again. You can test out these explanations in several ways. For example, you could ask a mutual friend for their take on the situation. Or you could invite your friends over for the evening and see how you all get on. You could even admit your worries to them, give them a call, and see how they react!

It isn't always easy to think of one single test that will give us convincing proof that a suspicious thought is true or not. But if we try out two or three it'll be easier to see which explanation seems most plausible.

Keep an open mind

This rule is perhaps the hardest of all, but also the most important.

Most of us want certainty most of the time. We want to know what's going on around us – and we want to understand it too. It's a way of feeling in control of our lives. And who doesn't want to feel in control?

But whether we like it or not, we all have to accept that there are some things we can't know for sure. Sometimes we just have to be comfortable with uncertainty.

It's especially important when you're dealing with suspicious thoughts. If an event or experience has been bothering you, think through the possible explanations and decide which, on the balance of the evidence, seems most likely to be true. But don't go chasing a certainty you may never achieve. Say, for example, a stranger on a bus stares at you in an unfriendly way. You might feel sure he was being hostile, but there's no way of knowing for certain what he was really thinking. A little doubt is a healthy thing – it's a sign that we're keeping our minds open rather than jumping to conclusions.

Now let's apply these five rules of good decision-making in Steps 7 and 8.

Step 7 Review the evidence

In Step 7 we want you to have a go at three exercises designed to help you think through the evidence for your suspicious thoughts.

Exercise A: Assessing the evidence for your main suspicious thought

First, write down the suspicious thought that's worrying you most:

Next rate how strongly you believe it (give a figure from 0 to 100 per cent):

Now use the table below to list the evidence that supports the thought – and the evidence that doesn't.

Evidence for:	Evidence against:

It's often difficult to think of the evidence against our suspicious thoughts – especially if those thoughts are causing us distress. If you're finding it hard, ask yourself these questions:

- *Is there anything that might suggest the thought could be wrong?*
- *What would my family or friends say if I talked to them about the thought? (It would actually be a great idea to ask them.)*
- *What would I say to a friend who came to me with a similar problem?*
- *What good things have happened to me that contradict the thought?*
- *Are there any alternative explanations for what seems to have happened?*
- *Are my thoughts based more on the way I feel than on solid evidence?*
- *Have I been jumping to conclusions?*
- *Am I exaggerating the chances of anything bad happening to me?*
- *Am I being over-sensitive?*
- *Am I misinterpreting things because I'm feeling anxious or down?*
- *If I was feeling happier would I still think of things in the same way?*
- *Are my past experiences getting in the way of me seeing the present situation clearly?*

After you've filled in the table, spend some time thinking about what you've written and then have another go at rating how strongly you believe the thought (from 0 to 100 per cent):

Exercise B: Assessing your suspicious thoughts over the course of a week

In Chapter 6 we asked you to keep a diary of your suspicious thoughts. You can use that diary to help you complete this exercise. What we want you to do is keep a record of your suspicious thoughts over the course of the week. Then, in much the same way as you did in the previous exercise, review the evidence for and against each of your thoughts. It's best to do this at a set time every day – that way it becomes a habit. In the column marked 'Rating', give a score from 0 to 100 per cent for how strongly you believe the thought after considering all the evidence for it.

Date	Suspicious thought	How strongly you believed it at the time (0–100%)	Evidence for	Evidence against	Rating after considering evidence (0–100%)

Here's an example from Keith's diary:

Date	Suspicious thought	How strongly you believed it at the time (0–100%)	Evidence for	Evidence against	Rating after considering evidence (0–100%)
Sunday 7th	They all hate me. They're against me.	90%	1 They look at me oddly. 2 I can see hate in their eyes. 3 They rarely come up and chat to me now. 4 On Friday I heard laughter when I left the room.	1 It's hard to be sure what people's expressions mean or to guess the thoughts in their heads – actually, my face probably doesn't look too friendly a lot of the time. 2 People have gone to lunch with me, and do sometimes ask me to the pub. 3 Most of the time nothing bad actually happens. 4 They could have been laughing at anything when I left the room. 5 Some of the lads are actually quite friendly towards me and always say 'Hello'.	20%

Exercise C: Assessing the alternative explanation

We've seen that our suspicious thoughts are caused by a combination of factors. In Chapter 6 we asked you to try filling in a diagram showing how your own suspicious thoughts are produced. Have a look at it now; you may well find that there's a lot of information in your diagram. It's probably not the simplest explanation you've ever come across! This isn't surprising – paranoia is a complex thing to explain. Because of this, it's often helpful to think of a phrase or two that sums up the key points you see in the diagram. Here are some examples:

- I'm safe now, just overly jumpy because of the past.
- I feel anxious but there is no actual danger.
- I'm a worrier.
- I'm always jumping to conclusions.
- The experiences I've had in the past have made me a bit over-sensitive.
- I dwell on things more than I should.
- I tend to get very stressed.
- My imagination runs away with me sometimes.
- I seem to always assume the worst in any situation.
- I'm not good at thinking of alternative explanations for stuff that happens.
- I read too much into people's expressions.
- I often feel vulnerable, but I know they're only feelings – they aren't facts.

When you look at the diagram you completed, what phrase comes to mind? Write it down here:

Have a look back at the diagram Emily produced on page 164. She was assessing her reaction to events at her colleague's leaving party. Emily summarised her diagram with the comments:

> *The way I react is pretty much determined by how stressed I am.*
>
> *I use any little thing to prove that my own sense of insecurity is justified.*

Emily's initial feeling had been that her suspicious thought had been caused by her colleague's behaviour – it was as simple as that. But these comments tell a different story. As the diagram shows, there's much more at work than first meets the eye.

Your diagram will probably also offer you a different story – an alternative explanation for your suspicious thoughts. Using the same scale as before (0–100 per cent), rate how strongly you believe this account:

Now we're going to apply the same sort of careful assessment to this alternative explanation as we did in the earlier exercises to the suspicious thoughts. Using the table below, jot down the evidence that supports the explanation and the evidence that doesn't. Take as much time as you need – try to really think through all the possibilities.

Evidence for:	**Evidence against:**

Once you've filled in the table, read it through and then reassess how strongly you believe it. Write down your new rating here:

When you look back at your alternative explanation, do you find it convincing? We hope that it provides a better account of your experiences than the suspicious thought. If it doesn't, you might need to make a few changes: have a look back at Chapters 4 and 5 to help you do this. And don't think of your alternative explanation as set in stone. As you think more about your experiences, and as new things happen in your life, revisit this alternative account and make the changes you think are right.

Step 8 Test your suspicious thoughts

Step 7 gives us the chance to see how likely it is that our suspicious thoughts have been correct. If the evidence seems to back them up, then we really may have been in danger. On the other hand, we may well find there's plenty of evidence to suggest that we've come to the wrong conclusion about what's going on.

Assessing the evidence for our thoughts like this is very useful, but it's *retrospective*. So instead of thinking back to things that have happened in the past, we want you to test out your suspicions on *new experiences*. Don't avoid the situations that trigger your paranoia – go looking for them and see whether your suspicion is actually warranted. Or alternatively, test out whether you are safe right now, irrespective of what may have happened in the past.

Testing out your fears like this can be a nerve-wracking experience. Don't try it until you've completed the previous steps and until you're sure that you're ready. It also means you'll have to drop your safety behaviours – the things we do to make it less likely that the thing we fear will actually happen. (If you want to refresh your memory on safety behaviours, have a look back at Chapters 3 and 5.) Testing your fears will involve putting yourself in situations that your safety behaviours would normally help you avoid.

Safety behaviours may appear to be saving us from harm, but they actually just keep our suspicious thoughts going. We may come to believe that our safety behaviours are the reason that nothing bad has happened to us – when actually it's because we're not really in danger.

Abandoning our safety behaviours isn't easy. It can seem as if we're dropping our guard and that disaster is bound to follow. If you feel this way, here are three tips to help you make the change:

- Take it slowly. Don't just give up all your safety behaviours in one go: do it gradually. Start by dropping the one you feel most comfortable losing and take it step by step from there.

- Think back to a time in your life when you managed quite happily without safety behaviours. Take heart from the fact that you coped in the past and have confidence that you'll be able to do so again in the future.
- Remind yourself of the real benefits you'll get from testing your fears. This isn't to say it won't be hard – it will be. But you have so much to gain. You'll get to see whether or not the paranoid thoughts that you've been struggling to deal with are justified. And doubtless you won't need us to tell you how big a difference that discovery could make to your life.

Devising your tests

If you're finding it hard to think of a good test for your suspicious thoughts, try to identify what it is that your thoughts are stopping you from doing. In Emily's case, her anxieties made her stay away from social events – and especially if they involved colleagues from work. She was sure that people didn't want to talk to her, so she was reluctant to join in a conversation. She thought people would just ignore her. For Emily, parties were places where people talked about her or laughed at her – and all behind her back. A glance in her direction meant a conversation about her; an overheard laugh meant a joke at her expense. She felt completely isolated. She was convinced she was being singled out and that no one else was being treated in the same way.

Emily tested her fears in four ways. Before she carried out each test, she predicted what would happen. And she rated her prediction from 0 to 100 per cent depending on how confident she was that it would prove to be correct. Here are Emily's four tests, her predictions and results:

1. **She would ask two friends whether they often noticed people glancing or staring at them.**

   Prediction Emily was 70 per cent sure that her friends wouldn't have experienced this.

   Result One friend said they'd been stared at lots of times and the other said it had occasionally happened.

2. **She would ask a trusted work colleague whether others minded her being at work social events.**

   Prediction She was 60 per cent certain that her colleague would say that people had been making negative comments about her.

   Result Emily's colleague was surprised by the question and said that people would like to see more of her. Emily had wondered whether her colleague would be totally honest, but she could see how genuinely surprised her colleague was and found this very reassuring.

3. **She would attend a work social event, join a group of people and try to be sociable.**

   Prediction Emily was 85 per cent sure that people wouldn't be friendly towards her and would soon move away.

   Result Some of the evening was difficult and Emily found it hard to join in at first, but she ended up in an interesting – and enjoyable – conversation. People were clearly friendly. They greeted her warmly, smiled and asked how she and her family were – and Emily felt more comfortable as the evening went on.

4. **She would invite colleagues out for the evening.**

   Prediction She was 100 per cent certain that no one would want to come to an event she'd arranged.

   Result Emily really had to pluck up her courage to do this and was very anxious about arranging the event. She started by mentioning the idea to the colleague she'd talked to in the first test. This helped her to ask all her other colleagues to a meal out. Most of the colleagues she invited attended, and afterwards one or two people even spontaneously said they should do it again soon.

Testing out your fears is a daunting task. It takes a lot of courage to put yourself in a situation where you'll feel at risk, so it's important to build up your confidence by starting with the relatively easy tests. You can then work your way up to the tests you find most difficult. This is what psychologists call a **hierarchy of tests**. It's a good idea, by the way, to repeat your tests. That way you're less likely to dismiss a positive outcome as a lucky fluke. The more you do the tests, the more confidence you'll have in the results. Your thoughts and memories of threat will recede and be replaced by new thoughts and memories of feeling safe.

Emily began with tests that involved gathering information by talking to other people. She moved on to doing things she would normally avoid – going out with work colleagues. Finally, she tackled the test she was most dreading and the one she was surest would end in disaster: organising a social event with colleagues.

When you're devising a set of tests, start by writing down a list of situations or activities you find difficult (for example, attending social events or walking home alone). Now arrange the list in order of difficulty (with the most difficult activity at the bottom). Write down the suspicious thought that is triggered or related to the situation or activity:

	Situation/activity	**Suspicious thought**
1		
2		
3		
4		

Here's Emily's list:

	Situation/activity	Suspicious thought
1	Share my experiences with friends.	My suspicions will be confirmed: no one else has these kinds of things happen to them at work. Friends will think I'm mad.
2	Ask someone at work about how other people see me.	People think I'm no good at my job. I'm not popular.
3	Try to socialise at work party.	People don't want to spend time with me and try to avoid me as much as possible. The senior staff definitely won't talk to me for long as they want me out.
4	Organise evening out.	People want me out of the company so they're hardly going to want to socialise with me.

Incidentally, don't put yourself in situations where you're likely to be at real risk. You may be worried about going out alone, but we don't recommend you test this by going into a dangerous neighbourhood at night. Concentrate instead on activities that most people would find reasonable and where you think your suspicious thoughts are probably exaggerated.

Aim for four or five tests. As you set about tackling them, keep a record of how you get on. Make sure you note down the following details for each test:

Suspicious thought to be tested:	
How strongly do I believe it (from 0 to 100%)?	
Test:	
My prediction:	
How sure am I of my prediction (from 0 to 100%)?	
Result of the test:	
My conclusions:	
How strongly do I believe the suspicious thought now (from 0 to 100%)?	
How strongly do I believe that I am safe from harm (from 0 to 100%)?	

Testing your fears can be tough, and it doesn't always go smoothly for everyone. It can really raise anxiety levels at first. The trick is to hang in there and let the anxiety diminish – which it will do over half an hour or so. Sometimes a test can just be too difficult. If that happens to you, go back to doing a test you find less stressful. Don't give up on testing completely, though. In our experience, people find it extremely helpful. After all, there's no better way to see how closely your suspicious thoughts match up to reality. You may well discover that they don't match up at all. And when that happens, you'll find that all kinds of activities you've been shying away from are suddenly open to you again.

Chapter summary

- This chapter covers Steps 7 and 8 of the ten practical steps that will help you overcome your suspicious thoughts.
- Suspicious thoughts are our interpretations of the things that happen to us.
- We need to review and challenge those interpretations rather than just accepting them, since things may now be different.
- We can review our suspicious thoughts and relearn feelings of safety by:
    - Assessing the evidence both for and against them.
    - Testing out our fears.

11

Coping with paranoid and suspicious thoughts as they happen

Introduction

One of the key lessons we want you to take from this book may seem a bit deflating: *suspicious thoughts are a part of life*. We all have them at some time or other, and it's likely that we always will. Life is full of moments when we have to decide whether or not to trust other people, and inevitably we'll sometimes make a mistake.

We can't help you avoid suspicious and paranoid thoughts for the rest of your life because it's simply not possible. What we can help you to do, though, is learn to cope with them – to manage them in such a way that they don't distress you and they don't affect your day-to-day life.

The practical steps we've set out will take you a long way toward this goal. Steps 1 and 2 are all about making sure you really understand your suspicious thoughts – and so don't need to fear them. Steps 3, 4, 5 and 6 get you to the right place to tackle the suspicions head on. Steps 7 and 8 are designed to help you test out those thoughts and to see just how accurate they really are. If you've had a go at these steps, you're probably aware that your suspicions are exaggerated. You're not really in the kind of danger you've been afraid of. Instead, you're gradually relearning safety.

Steps 1 to 8 will certainly help you deal with your suspicious thoughts. But what about the moment when the thought first occurs to you? If you're like most people paranoid thoughts happen when you're in a stressful situation. So it's not surprising if, when the thought occurs, all the knowledge you may have built up about what's causing your suspicious thoughts and how to deal with them goes right out of your head. Later, when you're nice and calm, you're able to remind yourself that your fears have always proved to be wrong. But it's another matter in the heat of the moment.

Step 9 will help you deal with your suspicious thoughts as they happen. We'll show you some techniques and strategies to use when you get the thought. In Step 10 you'll review what you've learned from this book and jot down your action plan for dealing with your suspicious thoughts.

Step 9 Dealing with your suspicious thoughts as they happen

Coping with suspicious thoughts really boils down to being in the right state of mind. Now you're probably wondering 'How on earth do I do that?' After all, it's hard to keep a positive attitude when you're dealing with what can be pretty upsetting thoughts.

But you can *learn* how to get yourself into this state of mind – and Step 9 presents four techniques to help you do just that. We can't promise an overnight transformation. If suspicious thoughts have been causing you problems, changing the way you react to them isn't going to be easy. But stick with it: given time and practice these techniques will really make a difference.

1 Don't fight the suspicious thought

White elephants.

For the next sixty seconds, we want you to *avoid thinking about white elephants*. Keep your mind completely free of them – and if a white elephant seems to be creeping in, suppress the thought as quickly as you can. Probably white elephants aren't something you normally give a lot of thought to so this should be easy, right? Off you go . . .

We're willing to bet that thoughts of white elephants kept on occurring no matter how hard you tried to put them out of your mind. That's certainly what happened when we tried this exercise. This isn't surprising: lots of research has shown that trying *not* to think about something only makes us think about it more.

So when you get a suspicious thought, don't fight it. Don't try to pretend it hasn't happened. Don't try to force it out of your mind. It'll only come back, just like those white elephants.

There's another reason why we shouldn't try to suppress a suspicious thought: we don't need to. It isn't giving us news we'd rather forget; it isn't a fact. It's just one of the thousands of thoughts we have each day, and we should treat it just like we do any of the others.

2 Let go of the suspicious thought

When a suspicious thought occurs, don't try to pretend it hasn't happened. Notice it – and then let it go.

Don't spend time thinking about the thought. Don't bother trying to understand it, and definitely don't act on it. Try to be detached – as if you're watching something happen to someone else long ago. Watch the thought come to you, remind yourself that it doesn't matter and let it fade into the distance.

For some people the suspicious thoughts can come in waves, one after the other. If this happens to you don't let those waves drag you down: try to ride them out. Don't let the thoughts upset you and don't try to make them stop coming. We know this is hard, but aim to stay as calm as you can. Hang on in there and watch the waves of thoughts fade into the distance.

You'll notice here there's a change of focus in our approach. Steps 1, 2, 7 and 8 were all about *analysing and understanding* your suspicious thoughts. If this has gone well, you'll have realised that your thoughts are probably exaggerated. So now it's time to shift gears and let the thoughts go without all that analysis.

3 Give yourself plenty of advice and encouragement

People often find it helpful to have a phrase or two they can repeat to themselves when they're experiencing suspicious thoughts. Obviously, that phrase should be a positive one! Think of the advice and encouragement you'd offer a friend who was having these thoughts – and then offer it to yourself. Or imagine what someone you admire might say. Tell yourself you're doing well and that you're going to see off these thoughts; or remind yourself of the key lessons you've learned from reading this book.

Here are some phrases we've seen used with good results:

- I'm just being over-sensitive.
- They're only thoughts – they don't matter.
- People are generally good – I'm safe.
- Keep going – you're doing really well.
- I'm jumping to conclusions again. There's no way I can know what she's thinking.
- It's just another of those thoughts – it'll pass.
- These thoughts don't scare me. I can cope.

It can be hard to remember this stuff in the middle of a paranoid thought so you might want to write down your key phrases on a card or bit of paper or on your mobile phone. You could print out a picture or photo that will lift your spirits and keep you motivated. Carry this material with you and it'll always be there when you need it.

Now, write down a phrase you think will help you deal with your suspicious thoughts.

4 Focus on what you're doing, not what you're thinking

Suspicious thoughts occur in all kinds of situations. We might be at a party, or at the cinema, or in a meeting at work. Wherever we happen to be we can get lost in our thoughts, completely forgetting whatever it is we're doing.

We have to make sure we don't get absorbed in our worries like this: all it does is increase their grip on us. Focus on the task in hand – your conversation with friends at the party, for example, or the film you're watching. Don't let your paranoid thoughts fool you into believing that they are the most important thing going on. Immerse yourself in what you're *doing*, rather than what you're thinking.

Of course suspicious thoughts also come to us when we're not doing anything very much. In fact, for many people they are *more likely* to occur when they don't have anything else to hold their attention. When we look back at the extract from Keith's diary in Chapter 6, we can see that it's really *only* when he's not doing a lot that his paranoid thoughts surface: watching TV, reading the paper, lying in bed, ironing. All of these situations are ones in which it's easy for the mind to wander. And most people's minds tend to wander back to their preoccupations . . . So if you're not doing much when you have a suspicious thought, try to put the thought to one side and get on with doing something you really enjoy.

Like many of the other techniques we set out in this book, these four strategies need practice and preparation. So now think of a typical situation in which you experience suspicious thoughts. How would you like yourself to react if a paranoid thought occurs? Visualise the thought occurring and your response to it. Don't worry about how you're actually likely to react, or how you've reacted in the past. Concentrate instead on your *ideal* reaction.

When you've visualised the scene, it's a good idea to write it down: it'll be a useful reminder of how you'd like to react in the future. Here's the note Keith wrote:

> *Sat at home watching TV on Sunday afternoon. Daydreaming. Started worrying about work. We always have team meetings on a Monday morning. Feel like these are turning into a chance for the boss to pick on me. Usually these thoughts prey on me. I can spend hours (or at least what feels like hours) turning them over in my mind. This time, though, I didn't let it get to me. I just told myself that it's what I always end up thinking on a Sunday afternoon, that it doesn't matter, and that I can't be bothered spending more energy on it. Said to myself a few times: 'It's just the usual nonsense. It'll be gone in a minute or so.' Then I got up off the sofa and went and rang my eldest to fix up a time for when I could go and visit her.*

You can see in Keith's description how he doesn't try to pretend that the thought hasn't happened. Instead of fighting it he stays calm and manages to get some distance from the experience. In fact, it's almost as if he were watching it happen to someone else. He gives himself some words of encouragement and advice and then makes sure he focuses on something that really absorbs him – planning to see his daughter.

Now have a go at writing your own account of how you'd ideally react to your suspicious thoughts.

Step 10 Staying well

If you've tried all nine of the steps described in the past five chapters you'll doubtless be relieved to know that we've not got any more up our sleeve! The exercises can be very hard work, for sure. But, all being well, they'll have been worth the effort.

If you *have* found them helpful, there's just one more little task we'd like you to have a go at. No matter how hard we work at dealing with our suspicious thoughts, we can't hope to get rid of them completely. At some point we're bound to have those feelings again – and we might find it hard to cope. It's usually easier to deal with problems if we've prepared a plan in advance, and that's what we want you to write now. Have a think about what you'd do if you were finding it hard to cope with paranoid thoughts in the future. Psychologists give this the not very optimistic name of a **relapse plan**; we prefer to call it an **action plan**.

To help you put together your own action plan, write down:

- The sorts of stresses and problems that are likely to trigger your suspicious thoughts.
- The early warning signs that these thoughts are getting to you (maybe you're drinking more, sleeping less well or feeling less like socialising).
- The steps you'll take to deal with these early troubling suspicious thoughts.

Make sure you keep this action plan somewhere safe – and somewhere you can easily find it in case you need it in the future.

Here's the action plan Keith came up with:

> ***Triggers:*** *Things that make me feel alone – for instance, the anniversary of my parents' deaths. Or if something happens at work – maybe someone new starting who isn't very friendly or if colleagues are laughing at a joke I don't get. I need to be careful with these sorts of things.*
>
> ***Warning signs:*** *Worrying is always the biggest sign for me. And wanting to spend less time with other people. Also feeling unsettled and stressed. If I'm not sleeping, that's usually a sign that things are getting worse.*

> ***What I'll do:*** *I'll definitely look at the book again for ideas. Starting worry periods again will help. Will also plan some good things (maybe catching up with the kids). And I'll try to talk to someone about my worries. The trick is going to be to catch things early, improve my mood, and not get caught up in my suspicious thoughts.*

If you've made it all the way through this book – and especially if you've tried the exercises – you can feel rightly proud of your efforts. We hope you'll now have a much greater understanding of suspicious thoughts: where they come from, why they can cause so much distress, and – most importantly – how they can be beaten.

Now might be a good time to revisit the exercise in Step 1 in Chapter 6. They will help you assess what your experience of suspicious thoughts is like now – and naturally we hope you'll see that it's much improved from when you started this book!

We hope that suspicious thoughts have become a much smaller part of your life, that in your own mind you are less defined by them, and that you have control over your reactions to them. If you want to know more about the issues we've discussed in this book, or if you feel you'd like more help, check out the information in Appendix 1.

Chapter summary

- Coping with suspicious thoughts is all about being in the right state of mind.
- When a suspicious thought comes to you, try to:
    - avoid fighting the thought or pretending it hasn't happened.
    - let it go: be as calm and detached as you can.
    - remind yourself what you're trying to achieve and give yourself plenty of encouragement.
    - focus on what you're *doing* and not what you're *thinking*.
- Make sure you write down an **action plan** to help you deal with suspicious thoughts if they get out of hand again in the future.

Appendix 1: Getting more help

This book is all about helping you cope with your suspicious thoughts. You'll know the trouble and distress these thoughts can cause. But now we hope you'll also see how you can put them behind you and get on with the rest of your life.

If you're still having problems with paranoid thoughts after having worked with this book, you may feel you want to consider other sources of help – perhaps seeing a therapist or trying medication. You might just want to find out a bit more about the issues. So here we set out the options for additional help and also include details of relevant organisations.

Professional help

You may have grown tired by now of our reminder that everyone experiences suspicious thoughts from time to time! However, only a small proportion of us ever see a doctor about them. So how do we know when it's right to ask for professional help?

There's no cut-and-dried answer to this one, but basically it boils down to:

- How distressing you're finding the thoughts.
- How much they're disrupting your life.

If the thoughts are making you feel very anxious or down, or if they're stopping you from functioning as you'd like to, then you may well want to think about seeking professional help. You should definitely do so if you're feeling very depressed or even suicidal.

That said, even if your suspicious thoughts aren't having an especially severe effect, they can still be unsettling. So though you might be coping, you might nonetheless find it helpful to talk things over with your doctor, see a therapist or try out some medication. You may also want a doctor to check to see whether your suspicious thoughts might be caused by one of the medical conditions we mentioned in Chapter 2 (see pages 61–66).

Sometimes we're just too close to the situation to know whether or not we need help. Talk things over with trusted friends or relatives: they'll be able to give their perspective on how your paranoid thoughts are affecting you.

If you do decide to seek professional help it's crucial that you find the right person. If you think your GP doesn't understand paranoid thoughts and their treatment, ask to be referred to a specialist. It's relatively easy to get knowledgeable advice on medication, but harder to find someone with specialist psychological knowledge – though the information given here should help.

Cognitive Behavioural Therapy (CBT)

There are lots of types of psychological therapy (also called 'psychotherapy' or 'talking therapy'). But the therapy that has been proved to be highly effective in dealing with suspicious thoughts – and the one that we draw upon throughout this book – is **Cognitive Behavioural Therapy** (CBT for short).

CBT is a *collaborative* therapy. You and your therapist will work together to:

- Agree the goals of the therapy;
- Identify the causes of your distress;
- Decide on strategies for reducing that distress.

You can expect the therapist to share their knowledge with you, and to regularly monitor your progress, but it's definitely *not* a case of the therapist simply telling you what the problem is and what you should do about it.

How many sessions of CBT will you need? Well, that's something you will work out with your therapist but most people have around ten to twenty weekly sessions. You can expect the therapy to draw on the sorts of strategies and thinking we present in this book, but there are other benefits. For a start, most people find that having the opportunity to discuss their problems with a sympathetic and knowledgeable person is a real positive. The structure of weekly appointments can really boost your motivation, and your therapist will be able to help you with the exercises and may well spot things you're unaware of. They may also be able to help with other problems you may have.

CBT therapists

CBT is mainly provided by clinical psychologists, though more and more psychiatrists, counselling psychologists, counsellors and nurses are becoming trained in this approach.

Clinical psychologists have studied psychology at university and then completed a three-year postgraduate degree. Most also have a doctoral degree in clinical psychology (meaning that they use the word 'Doctor' before their name). Clinical psychologists apply psychological theories and research to problems and don't prescribe medication.

Psychiatrists have trained as medical doctors and then gone on to specialise in the care of people with mental health problems. Their first line of treatment is usually medication, but some psychiatrists are also trained in psychological therapies such as CBT.

Defining the term 'counsellor' is trickier. It's a title used by people with widely differing types and amounts of training. Chartered counselling psychologists, for example, have studied for several years, obtained a doctoral degree and are often very similar to clinical psychologists. Some counsellors have extensive training but not in CBT. Others have only attended short courses. When you're looking for a counsellor, check that they've been properly trained, that they're a specialist in CBT and that they belong to an appropriate professional body. A number of organisations keep registers of CBT therapists (for example, the British Association for Behavioural and Cognitive Psychotherapies), and you can find details of these in the list of useful organisations below.

Getting CBT

If you want to explore the options for getting CBT, it's usually best to talk first to your family doctor (called a GP or General Practitioner in the UK). Your doctor has a good general knowledge of common illnesses and will be able to advise you on access to local resources and refer you to a therapist if appropriate. It's important that you're referred to a therapist who has been properly trained in the use of CBT: ask your doctor if you're not sure.

If you're feeling stressed, depressed or anxious, or if you're experiencing trouble sleeping, you can get help from the UK's excellent Improving Access to Psychological Therapies (IAPT) programme. You don't need a referral from your doctor; you can get in touch with the programme yourself. IAPT offers talking treatments such as CBT – treatments that have been proven to work for these kinds of problems.

IAPT is provided by local NHS services – usually, and a bit confusingly, under different names in different locations.

In Oxford, for example, it's called Talking Space Oxford (www.talkingspaceoxfordshire.org). To find the service in your area, visit http://www.nhs.uk/Service-Search/Psychological-therapies-(IAPT)/LocationSearch/10008.

In the UK most CBT therapists work in the National Health Service. Alternatively you may want to consider seeing a private therapist. Sometimes private therapy can be arranged by your GP. If not, you may need to find a therapist on your own. As ever, make sure your therapist is properly qualified (see the list of useful organisations below for help with this).

Medication

Medication is often prescribed for people who are suffering with severe paranoid thoughts and many of them find it helps. Remember that psychologists and counsellors can't prescribe medication; only GPs and psychiatrists can do so. As part of the consultation, they'll want to investigate possible physical causes of the suspicious thoughts. For example, they may take a blood sample so they can check for infection and see how your liver, kidneys and thyroid gland are functioning.

Two major categories of medication are given to combat paranoid thoughts:

- Antipsychotics.
- Anti-depressants.

Each of these two categories includes lots of different individual drugs. Finding out about these drugs can be a confusing business because they all have at least two names. Each drug has an official medical name (its *generic* name) and the *trade* name given by the company that makes it. For example, the drug fluoxetine is widely known by the trade name Prozac. We use the generic names in this Appendix.

Everyone responds differently to particular drugs so it may take time to find the right medication and the right dose. Each drug also has its own set of potential side-effects and risks. Your doctor will discuss with you how you're getting on with the medication they've prescribed and may alter the dose or even the drug until you find the one that's most effective. Make sure your doctor explains:

- How much of the medication to take and how often;
- The potential side-effects;
- How you'd go about stopping the medication, if that's what you eventually decide (for example, it's often best to reduce the amount you take gradually rather than immediately stopping altogether).

Antipsychotics

Antipsychotics are one of the two major types of drug prescribed for suspicious thoughts. They're sometimes called 'neuroleptics' or 'major tranquillisers'. Antipsychotics are mainly prescribed for people with mental health problems such as schizophrenia or psychosis, but in smaller doses they're sometimes used to treat anxiety and agitation.

Antipsychotics take a few days or weeks to act. If one doesn't work, doctors often try one of the others. There are lots of antipsychotic medications available now. The older ones include chlorpromazine, haloperidol and trifluoperazine. Among the newer ones, often called 'atypical neuroleptics', are risperidone, amisulpride, olanzepine and clozapine. If your doctor suggests an antipsychotic, it's likely to be a low dose of an atypical.

The downside of antipsychotics is the unpleasant and occasionally severe side-effects they can produce, including drowsiness, weight gain, reduced sexual desire and diabetes.

Anti-depressants

Your doctor may feel that your suspicious thoughts will reduce if your mood is better. In this case, they'll probably prescribe an anti-depressant. There are various types of anti-depressants, but chances are you'll be given one of the newer *SSRIs* (or 'selective serotonin reuptake inhibitors').

Commonly used SSRIs are fluoxetine, paroxetine, citalopram and sertraline. As with neuroleptics, it may be a while before the SSRI starts working. However, the side-effects (for example, stomach upset, agitation, rashes, reduced sexual desire) are usually less common and less severe than those caused by neuroleptics.

The other commonly prescribed type of anti-depressants is the *tricyclics* – examples include amitryptyline, imipramine and clomipramine. SSRIs are thought to have fewer side-effects than the tricyclic medications.

The website www.mentalhealthcare.org.uk lists responses to questions posted about medication to the Maudsley Hospital Chief Pharmacist.

Useful organisations

A number of health profession organisations and mental health charities provide information and support. Some of them also keep registers of cognitive therapists (though being listed doesn't mean a particular therapist is a specialist in suspicious thoughts). We list the organisations within a country alphabetically.

UK

British Association for Behavioural and
Cognitive Psychotherapies
Imperial House
Hornby Street
Bury
Lancashire BL9 5BN
Tel: 0161 705 4304
Email: babcp@babcp.com
www.babcp.org.uk
Lists accredited cognitive therapists.

British Psychological Society
St Andrews House
48 Princess Road East
Leicester LE1 7DR
Tel: 0116 254 9568
Email: enquiry@bps.org.uk
www.bps.org.uk
Lists chartered clinical psychologists.

The Mental Health Foundation
Colechurch House
1 London Bridge Walk
London SE1 2SX
Tel: 0207 803 1100
www.mentalhealth.org.uk

MIND (National Association for Mental Health)
15–19 Broadway
London E15 4BQ
Tel: 020 8519 2122
Information line tel: 0300 123 3393
Email: contact@mind.org.uk
www.mind.org.uk

Oxford Cognitive Therapy Centre
Warneford Hospital
Oxford OX3 7JX
Tel: 01865 902801
Email: octcsupport@oxfordhealth.nhs.uk
www.octc.co.uk

Rethink
89 Albert Embankment
London SE1 7TP
General enquiries tel: 0121 522 7007
Email: info@rethink.org
National Advice service tel: 0300 5000 927
Email: advice@rethink.org
www.rethink.org

The Royal College of Psychiatrists
21 Prescot Street
London E1 8BB
Tel: 0207 235 2351
Email: reception@rcpsych.ac.uk
www.rcpsych.ac.uk

SANE
St Mark's Studios
14 Chillingworth Road
Islington
London N7 8QJ
Tel: 020 3805 1790
SANELINE (helpline) tel: 0300 304 7000
Email: info@sane.org.uk
www.sane.org.uk

The South London and Maudsley NHS Foundation
Trust/Institute of Psychiatry, Psychology and
Neuroscience, King's College London
The Maudsley Hospital
Denmark Hill
London SE5 8AZ
http://www.slam.nhs.uk
http://www.kcl.ac.uk/ioppn/index.aspx
www.mentalhealthcare.org.uk

The Trust's PICuP Clinic provides CBT for severe paranoia and other distressing unusual experiences, as well as Family Interventions. NHS referrals must come from a GP or a community mental health team, although private patients can self-refer. The PICuP Clinic (Psychological Intervention Clinic for Outpatients with Psychosis) can be contacted on tel: 0203 228 3524, email: picup@slam.nhs.uk.

Europe
The European Association for Behavioural and Cognitive Psychotherapies (EABCT) website (www.eabct.eu) provides links to national cognitive therapy organisations in Europe (via its 'Find a Therapist' section). It lists, for example, the website for the Netherlands Association of Behaviour and Cognitive Therapy (which keeps a register of cognitive therapists): www.vgct.nl.

USA

Academy of Cognitive Therapy
245 N. 15th Street, MS 403
17 New College Building
Department of Psychiatry
Philadelphia
PA 19102
Email: info@academyofct.org
www.academyofct.org
Lists accredited cognitive therapists in the US and many other countries.

American Psychiatric Association
1000 Wilson Boulevard
Suite 1825
Arlington
VA 22209
APA Answer Centre tel: 1-888-35-PSYCH
From outside the US and Canada tel: 1-703-907-7300
Email: apa@psych.org
www.psych.org

American Psychological Society
750 First Street
NE, Washington
DC 20002-4242
Tel: (800) 374-2721 or (202) 336-5500
www.apa.org
Keeps a register of psychologists.

Beck Institute for Cognitive Therapy and Research
One Belmont Avenue, Suite 700
Bala Cynwyd
PA 19004-1610
Tel: 610-664-3020
Email: info@beckinstitute.org
www.beckinstitute.org

National Alliance for the Mentally Ill (NAMI)
3803 N. Fairfax Drive
Suite 100 Arlington
VA 22203
Information Helpline tel: 1-800-950-NAMI (6264)
www.nami.org

National Institute of Mental Health
6001 Executive Boulevard
Rockville
MD 20852
Tel: 301-443-8431 (local)
Tel: 1-866-615-6464 (toll-free)
Email: nimhinfo@nih.gov
www.nimh.nih.gov

National Mental Health Association (NMHA)
2001 N. Beauregard Street, 12th Floor
Alexandria
VA 22311
Tel: (703) 684-7722
www.nmha.org

Appendix 2: Further reading

This is the only self-help guide to dealing with suspicious thoughts, though you may be interested in *Paranoia: The Twenty-first Century Fear* by Daniel Freeman and Jason Freeman (Oxford University Press, 2008), which is a concise and accessible look at the prevalence and causes of paranoia in contemporary society. There are also many excellent books on related topics and we note some of these in the list below. But don't feel restricted to our suggestions: take the time to browse in a good bookshop or library and pick the book you find the most readable and helpful. Alternatively, online stores stock hundreds of self-help titles.

Anxiety

Gillian Butler, *Overcoming Social Anxiety and Shyness* (Robinson, 2016).

Daniel Freeman & Jason Freeman, *How to Keep Calm and Carry On: Inspiring Ways to Worry Less and Live a Happier Life* (Pearson, 2013).

Christine Ingham, *Panic Attacks* (HarperCollins, 2000).

Helen Kennerly, *Overcoming Anxiety* (Robinson, 2014).

Roz Shafran, Lee Brosan and Peter Cooper, *The Complete CBT Guide for Anxiety* (Robinson, 2013).

Chris Williams, *Overcoming Anxiety* (Hodder & Arnold, 2003).

Assertiveness

Gael Lindenfield, *Assert Yourself* (HarperCollins, 2001).

Depression

Lee Brosan & David Westbrook, *The Complete CBT Guide for Depression and Low Mood* (Robinson, 2015).

David Burns, *Feeling Good* (Avon Books, 2000).

Paul Gilbert, *Overcoming Depression* (Robinson, 2009).

Dennis Greenberger & Christine Padesky, *Mind Over Mood* (Guilford Press, 1995).

Chris Williams, *Overcoming Depression* (Hodder & Arnold, 2001).

Mark Williams, John Teasdale, Zindel Segal & Jon Kabat-Zinn, *The Mindful Way Through Depression* (Guilford, 2007).

Mental health

Gillian Butler & Tony Hope, *Manage Your Mind: The Mental Fitness Guide* (Oxford Paperbacks, 2007)

Daniel Freeman & Jason Freeman, *Know Your Mind: Everyday Emotional and Psychological Problems and How to Overcome Them* (Rodale, 2009).

Mark Williams & Danny Penman, *Mindfulness: A Practical Guide to Finding Peace in a Frantic World* (Piatkus, 2011).

Post-traumatic stress disorder

Claudia Herbert & Ann Wetmore, *Overcoming Traumatic Stress* (Robinson, 2008).

Aphrodite Matsakis, *I Can't Get Over It: Handbook for Trauma Survivors* (New Harbinger, 1996).

Relationships

Aaron Beck, *Love is Never Enough: How Couples Can Overcome Misunderstandings, Resolve Conflicts and Solve Relationship Problems Through Cognitive Therapy* (HarperCollins, 1989).

Michael Crowe, *Overcoming Relationship Problems* (Robinson, 2005).

Schizophrenia

Steven Jones & Peter Hayward, *Coping with Schizophrenia: A Guide for Patients, Families and Caregivers* (One World, 2004).

Elizabeth Kuipers & Paul Bebbington, *Living with Mental Illness: A Book for Relatives and Friends* (Souvenir Press, 2005).

Anthony Morrison, Julia Renton, Paul French & Richard Bentall, *Think You're Crazy? Think Again* (Routledge, 2008).

British Psychological Society, *Understanding Psychosis and Schizophrenia*. (BPS, 2014). This can be downloaded at:

http://www.bps.org.uk/networks-and-communities/member-microsite/division-clinical-psychology/understanding-psychosis-and-schizophrenia

Self-esteem

David Burns, *10 Days to Great Self-Esteem* (Vermilion, 2000).

Melanie Fennell, *Overcoming Low Self-Esteem* (Robinson, 2016).

Daniel Freeman & Jason Freeman, *You Can Be Happy* (Pearson, 2012).

Mathieu Ricard, *Happiness* (Little, Brown, 2007).

Sleep problems

Colin Espie, *Overcoming Insomnia and Sleep Problems* (Robinson, 2006).

Meir Kryger, *A Woman's Guide to Sleep Disorders* (McGraw-Hill, 2004).

Stress management

Lee Brosan & Gillian Todd, *Overcoming Stress* (Robinson, 2009)

Allen Elkin, *Stress Management for Dummies* (Hungry Minds, 2013).

Terry Looker & Olga Gregson, *Managing Stress* (Teach Yourself Books, 2003).

Stephen Palmer & Gary Cooper, *How to Deal with Stress* (Kogan Page, 2013).

Voices

Mark Hayward, Clara Strauss & David Kingdon, *Overcoming Distressing Voices* (Robinson, 2012).

Worry

Kevin Meares & Mark Freeston, *Overcoming Worry and Generalised Anxiety Disorder* (Robinson, 2015)

If you would like to provide feedback on *Overcoming Paranoid and Suspicious Thoughts* or would like to share your experiences with others, please visit: www.paranoidthoughts.com.

Follow @ProfDFreeman and @JasonFreeman100 on Twitter.

Index